Rational Individualism

A Moral Argument
for
Limited Government
and Capitalism

Michael A. Beitler, Ph.D.

PRACTITIONER PRESS INTERNATIONAL

Send inquires and orders for this book to:
P.O. Box 38353
Greensboro, NC 27438
information@ppi-bookstores.com
or
www.rationalindividualism.com

Library of Congress Control Number: 2008932541
1. Political Philosophy 2. Economics

ISBN 13: 978-0-9726064-3-1

Printed in the United States of America

I dedicate this book to my children,

Rebecca Grace

David Beitler

Stephen Beitler

Acknowledgements

I OWE AN INTELLECTUAL DEBT to my wife, Danyang (Danielle) Peng, and to my three children. In particular, I want to thank David Beitler, my eldest son, for patiently working with me to clarify the concepts in this book.

I also want to thank all of the individuals who have encouraged me to stand up for individual rights, limited government, and capitalism. They are too numerous to list here, but I am forever in their debt.

Table of Contents

Chapter 1

Individual Rights

SOCIALISM IS IMMORAL. Capitalism is the only moral political-economic system. The purpose of this book is to prove those two statements.

During my career of more than three decades, I have been a business executive, business consultant, business professor, and business author. I have had the opportunity to work with some of the most successful people in the world.

Successful People

My experiences with highly successful people were not what I had anticipated. Highly successful people have above-average intelligence, but they are not geniuses. They develop their innate abilities and work very hard. They drive themselves unrelentingly to succeed. This drive to succeed is self-imposed.

These highly successful people should feel a sense of pride. Most of them do not. Many of them feel guilty about their success. This guilt is not self-imposed. This guilt is imposed upon them by people of less ability and less initiative who are armed with the ideology of collectivism/statism/socialism.

In contrast, the ideology on which America was founded was individualism/libertarianism/capitalism. But in the early twenty-first century, America is abandoning its founding ideology.

Today, highly successful Americans are under attack simply for being successful. Since these highly successful people are doers, they rarely take the time to form an argument to refute their tormentors. This book offers a defense—a moral defense.

Successful people create jobs, make innovative products available to the masses, develop life-saving drugs and new technology, and invest their money in projects that benefit all of us.

Successful people make a lot of money. They should. They are the engines of progress, the heroes of society. They earn their money. Their money is their compensation for their creation of value.

Many successful people give large sums of their money to charity. However, they have absolutely no moral obligation to do so. Freedom and charity can co-exist in a free society only if charity is voluntary (rather than government-imposed).

Aggressive Panhandling

Everybody has been approached on the street by a beggar, somebody who is "down on his luck" or unemployed, asking for a handout. Most of us grab a few bucks out of our pocket, give them to him, and sincerely say, "Good luck." That's not the same thing as "aggressive panhandling."

Aggressive panhandling (illegal in many cities) is borderline mugging and involves intimidation. An aggressive panhandler is angry at us for being more successful than he is. He demands money from us. He believes we owe him something simply because we have more than he does.

I have seen this same deplorable behavior in the corporate world. For many years, I worked as a senior executive of a successful bank. Our management team often met with representatives of various charities and causes. We were often threatened. Even though we gave contributions to just about everybody, I always found the threats to be very disturbing. Aggressive panhandling techniques seemed "fair" to these fundraisers simply because we had more money than they had.

In the early twenty-first century, laws are being passed to prohibit aggressive panhandling on the streets, but the same techniques are growing more common in corporate boardrooms.

Legalized Extortion

In a free society, laws forbid extortion; in a socialist system extortion is legalized. One group "legally" extorts money from another group. They don't do it directly. The government, which can use force or the threat of force, serves as the collector of the extorted funds.

Legalized extortion and aggressive panhandling should never be confused with charity. Legalized extortion and aggressive panhandling are violations of our inalienable individual rights.

Individual Rights and Freedom

A free society must be based on individual rights. You are not free unless you have individual rights. Individual rights are the means of subordinating society to moral law. It is society that has to be subordinated. Otherwise individual rights will slowly, but surely, be forfeited to the state. A free society must have individual rights as the philosophical basis for every political and economic decision.

Individual rights are inalienable. When an individual is robbed or enslaved, the individual's rights are still inalienable. The right remains with the individual victim. The criminal (another individual, group, or state) has not acquired the right. The criminal's force may have succeeded in acquiring the victim's property, but not in acquiring the right to the property.

The fundamental individual right is the right to life. The right to life requires rights to liberty, property, and the pursuit of happiness. Nobody is free without these rights.

The right to liberty is the right to act in accordance with your own judgment. The right to property is the right to earn, keep, use, and dispose of your property as you see fit. The right to the pursuit of happiness is the right to pursue your own happiness based upon your own judgment.

These rights are necessary for freedom. These rights are inalienable.

Group Rights

The term "group rights" is a contradiction in terms. A group (government, organization, or any collective) has no rights. If a group has a right, it must have taken that right from an individual(s).

The advocate of group rights wants the power to decide who will be the beneficiaries and who will be the exploited. Any rights given to one individual or group must be taken from another. If a product or service is given free-of-charge to an individual or group, it must be taken by force, or the threat of force, from the productive work of another individual(s). This violates the rights of the productive individual(s).

Philosopher Ayn Rand once said, "A man can neither acquire new rights by joining a group nor lose the rights which he does possess. The principle of individual rights is the only moral base of all groups or associations."

Government Rights

Governments do not have rights. Governments of free societies are granted permissions from their citizens to enforce the laws that protect individual rights.

No government has the right to enslave. Free food for one part of the population means slave labor for the rest. It is wrong to turn the need of one individual or group into the responsibility (burden) of another. To do so violates the rights of the latter. The need of one individual does not constitute a claim on the earnings of another individual. (Don't get me wrong, I am glad to make a contribution to a worthy cause, but it's a charitable contribution—not a duty.)

Individual rights are not *from* the State (the government), but *against* the State. Individual rights are protection against others (including the State).

Violated Rights

Ayn Rand has said, "Rights can be violated only by the use of physical force," a significant statement because it allows for attempts to influence another person, but not to use physical force (or the threat of force) to coerce. Rational arguments and "sales pitches" are permissible in the marketplace of products, services, and ideas. Initiating physical force, or threatening physical force, is never permissible among free people.

You have the right to reject my product, service, or ideas. You do not have the right to silence me with physical force. You do have the right not to associate with me.

Property Rights

Without property rights, no other individual rights are possible. John Locke, an English philosopher, was an early Enlightenment writer who emphasized the importance of property rights. Locke's *Second Treatise on Civil Government*, published in 1690, offered the American Founding Fathers the guidance they needed to establish a free society without a monarch.

"Since man has to sustain his life by his own effort, the man who has no right to the product of his effort has no means to sustain his life" (Binswanger, 1986, p.388). It is the role of government to protect this right. (We will discuss the role of government in the next chapter.)

"The source of property rights is the law of causality. All property and all forms of wealth are produced by man's mind and labor" (Rand, 1961, p.182). It should be obvious, if an individual cannot keep the product of his/her efforts, that individual will not be motivated to produce. Can you see why protecting individual property rights is critical in a free and productive society?

Failure to protect property rights not only discourages productivity, it encourages theft ("legal" or otherwise). Ayn Rand offers the possibility of a government decreeing robbery as legal and resisting robbery as illegal (Rand, 1961, p.182). In such a society, all the citizens (all robbers at some point) will eventually starve to death because they will run out of prey. Productivity is a necessity in a society. Producers must be protected; robbers must be jailed.

Let's be clear about what we mean by property rights. We do not mean that people have a right to unearned property. Productive people are not obligated to give property to unproductive people. Right to property means the right to earned property. Once earned, you have the right to keep, use, and dispose of the property as you see fit.

The right to property necessitates the right of free trade. The right of free trade is the right to trade with another person without coercion. The right of free trade protects the voluntary exchange of value for value. Each individual's profit (benefit) is based upon his/her standard of value.

Conclusion

Throughout this book, I use the term "individual rights." I realize the term "individual rights" is redundant. Only the individual has rights. Governments and groups can have permissions, which are granted by individuals, but not rights.

References ———————————————————

Binswanger, Harry. (1986). *The Ayn Rand Lexicon*. New York: Meridian.

Rand, Ayn. (1961). *For the New Intellectual*. New York: Signet.

Chapter 2

Limited Government

As an individualist, libertarian, and capitalist, I believe it's critical that the role of government be limited.

As I write this book in the early twenty-first century, we see wealthy capitalist countries (including the United States) racing towards socialism. At the same time, communist and socialist countries (including China) are racing towards capitalism.

Great wealth was created during the capitalist era in the West, allowing the governments of Western countries to fund countless social programs. But now it's obvious that the financial weight of these programs is crushing these economies.

The governments of the socialist countries of Europe are increasing taxes on productive people to support government programs for unproductive people. This act is immoral—extorting money from productive people for the benefit of the unproductive. "Legalized" extortion is not a proper role of government.

The problem with any socialist state is the continuous expansion of the role of government. The recipients of "government money" will always want more, and will believe they have been cheated if "their money" is reduced. The bureaucrats who administer these programs have a vested interest in expanding the programs too. The more "government money" they give away, the more "government money" they receive.

In reality, there is no such thing as "government money." Money represents value. Value must be created through the production of goods or services. So-called government money is money that was earned by working people, not government employees. Government employees owe a fiduciary responsibility to the people who earned it—the taxpayers.

Am I saying that I am anti-government? Am I saying that I am against taxation? No and no. But before we can discuss the proper levels of funding (taxation), we must be clear about the proper role of government in a free society.

The Proper Role of Government

The proper role of government is to protect the rights of its individual citizens. This is necessarily true for a free society. Any other role of government requires the usurping of individual rights.

In contrast to the free society, there is the "statist" society. In a statist society (socialist, fascist, or communist), power is acquired by the State at the expense of individual rights. Keep in mind that groups do not have rights. Any group or collective "right" has to be usurped from individuals.

The role of government in a statist society is based upon the assumption that the individual has no rights. The individual in such societies has no rights; he or she has only "permissions" granted by the state. In a statist society the individual's only justification for living is to serve the state. Nazi Germany and Soviet Russia are the clearest examples in recent history, but statist governments have existed throughout history around the world. These countries started their downward spiral into statist regimes by using expressions such as "king above self," "country above self," or "the interest of fellow citizens above self."

Regardless of the rhetoric used, the result is always the same. Individual rights are usurped and put into the hands of government bureaucrats. The state becomes everything; the individual becomes nothing.

In a free society, government is the servant. In a free society, government is the protector of individual rights. To protect the rights of its citizens, the government in a free society has three basic roles:

- the military
- the police force
- the court systems

Government has a legitimate need for funding to fulfill these roles. Any funding (taxation) beyond these three basic functions must be clearly justified as to how it protects individual rights. Any individual or government agency receiving taxpayer funds has a fiduciary responsibility to the taxpayers. Anybody violating this fiduciary responsibility should be punished by dismissal and/or imprisonment.

Obviously, following these basic principles would dramatically reduce the size of government and the tax burden on working people. At the same time, following these principles would restore many of the individual rights that have already been forfeited to the State.

Since it is the role of government to protect individual rights against force, the government must be empowered to use force. The government serves as the individual's agent. Philosopher Ayn Rand believed individuals must agree to delegate their right of self-defense (except during emergencies) to government officials. If individuals are allowed to exact their own revenge, society would quickly deteriorate into anarchy. Try to imagine Dodge City in the television show *Gunsmoke* without Marshal Dillon.

Obviously, giving weapons to government officials is a serious matter. It must be constantly preached that government is the servant of individual citizens, not the other way around. Government's fiduciary responsibility to its citizens cannot be overemphasized. Government's power must be limited to retaliation against aggression. Its power is derived from the individual's right to life, liberty, property, and the pursuit of happiness. Government never has the right to initiate aggression.

"The use of force against one man," states Ayn Rand, "cannot be left to the arbitrary decision of another." Peikoff (1993, p.364) adds, "Every aspect of the retaliatory use of force must be defined in advance, validated, codified: under what conditions force can be employed, by whom, against whom, in what forms, to what extent."

Placing retaliatory force under government control is an attempt to place it under objectively defined laws. Government, therefore, must be a government of laws, not of individual preferences or whim.

Peikoff (1993, p.364) correctly states, "Since rational laws prohibit only crimes defined in terms of specific physical acts (force), the individual is able to know, prior to taking action, whether or not the law forbids it and what the consequences of disobedience will be." The interpretation of such laws must not be subject to individual whim. Peikoff goes on to say, "This stands in stark contrast to laws forbidding crimes against 'blasphemy,' 'obscenity,' or 'unfair profits.'" Laws against blasphemy, obscenity, or unfair profits are subject to whim because they are not defined as specific acts. The law must make clear what acts are forbidden.

As I mentioned earlier, one important function of government is the court systems. Even between two honorable people, disagreements arise. Each person may sincerely believe a promise has been broken or that he/she has been harmed. It's the role of the courts to settle such disputes. The government's role is to determine which laws apply and how to settle the dispute. The government's role as impartial judge helps defuse emotionally charged parties, who may be tempted to resort to physical force. Here again, the government must apply objective laws. Judges must not use their positions to promote their own agendas or preferences.

What the Government is Not

Peikoff (1993) states, "[T]he state must not intervene in the intellectual or moral life of its citizens" (p.367). Further, "Its function is to protect freedom, not truth or virtue" (p.367).

Individual rights include the rights to think and act as you see fit. This means you have the right to think and act irrationally. Unless you violate the rights of others, the government (police, military, or court system) must not intervene.

I must admit that I become personally frustrated when I see people thinking or acting irrationally, but it's not my right to stop them. Likewise, government (our agent with a monopoly on physical force) must never attempt to enforce ideas (right or wrong). A government that does so is the enemy, not the protector, of freedom.

Government and Business

We constantly hear about calls for government to regulate trade. But what right does government have to "regulate" trade? Government is empowered to protect individual rights and should intervene when individual rights have been violated. If "regulate" means oversee and control, that's clearly not the role of government.

What government bureaucrat, even a well-meaning one, is qualified to determine good business practice? Traders in the marketplace have always been able to regulate trade. In fact, you can't stop the traders from regulating trade. If you sell a bad product, or charge too much for your service, you'll be out-of-business long before the government can react. The marketplace is much more efficient than government.

The role of government in the marketplace is to protect individual rights.

Every individual trader is responsible for his/her own sustenance. Government must not intervene (with taxpayer money and resources) to prop-up weak businesses. There are at least four reasons why it is wrong to do so:

1. It's a violation of the government's fiduciary responsibility to the taxpayers. The taxpayers are not responsible for someone's incompetence and inefficiency.

2. It's unfair to the efficient, well-run businesses that offer valuable products and services at competitive prices.

3. Inefficient businesses do not have rights to life; only individuals do.

4. Inefficient businesses do not have rights to the property of others.

If you want to read some outrageous attempts by government to intervene in businesses that have wasted millions of dollars, read John Stossel's (2004) book, *Give Me A Break.*

Awesome Power

The government is granted enormous power by its citizens. This awesome power becomes frightening when it's abused. Any individual using government power for personal gain must be punished severely and publicly. Throughout history, countless evil people have been attracted to government power because of its potential for financial gain and power over others. One of the roles of the news media in a free society is to alert citizens to the danger of such people.

Government Rights?

Peikoff (1993, p.368) states, "In a proper society, the citizens have rights, but the government does not. The government acts by permission, as expressed in a written constitution that limits public officials to defined functions and procedures." This distinction between rights and permissions is critical. The government is granted permissions based upon the rights of the individuals it protects. These permissions can be revoked.

Government should be empowered to perform its legitimate role of protecting individual rights. But an empowered government still has no rights. A collective (any group, including government) can be empowered to act as the agent for individuals, but only individuals have rights.

If a society is to remain free, it must control its government. A free society must place clear limits on its government's power. Since government has no rights, government officials must know specifically what they are permitted to do. Ayn Rand once summarized this concept by saying, "A private individual may do anything except that which is legally forbidden; a government official may do nothing except that which is legally permitted." If we keep her one-sentence summary in mind, the proper role of government remains clear.

Does this mean that government is to be severely restricted? Yes. If not, the government will become the enemy of the people, rather than the protector. Government must remain the servant (not the ruler) while individuals exercise their rights.

Democracy or Republic

The Founding Fathers of the United States did not envision a democracy but a republic. A democracy with unlimited majority rule is dangerous. You should be concerned if you live under a democracy with unlimited majority rule. It means your individual rights are not protected. In such a society, your rights can be taken away by a majority vote.

"A republic, by contrast, is a system restricted to the protection of individual rights. In a republic, majority rule applies only to some details. Rights, however, remain an absolute; i.e., the principles governing the government are not subject to vote" (Peikoff, 1993, pp.368-369).

Anarchism

Whenever I speak about government, somebody will ask, "What do you think of anarchists?" I always respond, "I think they're crazy."

I want to live in a free society. Government plays an important role in a free society. Government's legitimate role in a free society is to protect individual rights.

In anarchies there is nobody to protect your individual rights.

Imagine living in the Dodge City of the *Gunsmoke* television show. You would need to wear a gun at all times to protect yourself. You must also be good with your gun because at any time a drunken cowboy can challenge you to a gunfight. If you are lucky, you are in the Long Branch Saloon where Marshal Dillon is having a beer with Miss Kitty and Doc. Marshal Dillon steps in to break up the fight. Since he is a foot taller than both of you, wears a badge, and is fast with his gun, your challenger walks toward the swinging doors. But as he leaves he looks back at you and promises, "You dirty prairie rat, I'll kill you if it's the last thing I do."

Now, imagine living in Dodge City without Marshal Dillon. That's anarchy.

In a peaceful society there must be a way to settle disputes between its members. Government serves that purpose. Anarchists fail to recognize that honest disagreement and deliberate evil will always exist. Individuals need a government (controlled by strict laws) for protection. Anarchy invariably leads to gangs and warlords who promise protection.

Where I Stand

Whenever I speak about government I am invariably asked, "So, where do you stand?" I always answer, "I'll stand with anybody who has his or her individual rights violated."

That answer is never a satisfactory answer. Every group demands to know where I stand politically on a horizontal line with liberals on the extreme left and conservatives on the extreme right.

One questioner walked to the blackboard and drew the following line with communism on the left and fascism on the right.

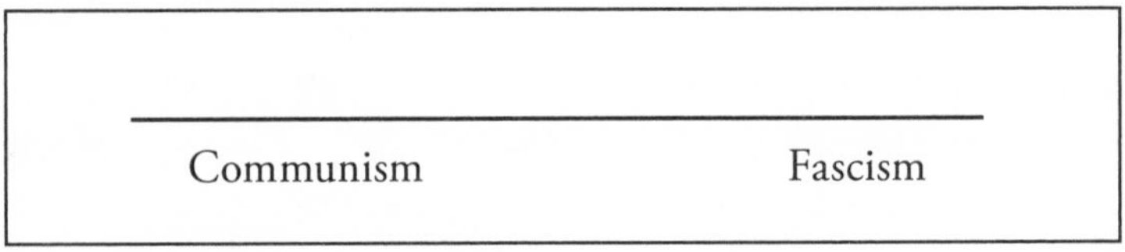

Communism   Fascism

FIGURE I

He then handed me the chalk and commanded me to put a dot on the line to indicate where I stood.

I told him that I was totally opposed to everything on that horizontal line: communism, fascism, and everything in between.

I then said, "If you want me to put a dot on a line, I will need to draw a vertical line as well." I drew the following vertical line with individualism at the top and statism at the bottom.

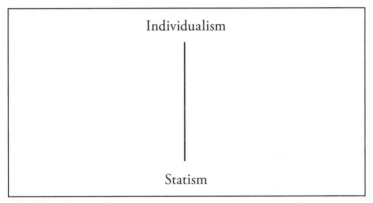

Individualism

Statism

FIGURE 2

I then told him that anything on his horizontal line (plus theocracies, absolute monarchies, democratic socialism, and dictatorships) would soon collapse into statism.

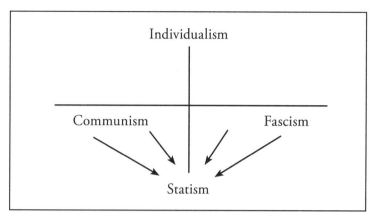

FIGURE 3

I am against every possible system along that the horizontal line because every one of them ultimately becomes a statist/socialist system. Statism and socialism, by their nature, violate individual rights. The state can only acquire rights by usurping them from individuals.

It is impossible to look at Stalin's Soviet Socialism in Russia or Hitler's National Socialism in Germany and believe these systems could have led to a free society with individual rights. In these socialist societies individuals had no rights to life, liberty, property, or the pursuit of happiness. The individual in a socialist society is the property of the collective (the State).

We now have countless examples of the horrors of socialism. Socialism (with all-powerful State control) did not end with the fall of Nazi Germany or the collapse of Soviet Russia. North Korea, Cuba, and the leftist regimes of South America are continuing examples of socialist societies where individuals live without rights.

Thomas Jefferson said the natural tendency is for the government to grow at the expense of individual liberty. Many of us today are so busy we don't detect the slow erosion of our individual rights.

The importance of standing up for individual rights cannot be overemphasized. Americans, including me, must stand against the erosion of our individual rights. That's where I stand.

References

Peikoff, Leonard. (1993). *Objectivism*. New York: Meridian.

Stossel, John. (2004). *Give Me a Break*. New York: Harper Collins.

CHAPTER 3

Capitalism

"CAPITALISM IS NOT merely the *practical*, but the only moral system in history," said Ayn Rand (1967, p.ix). That seems like a very bold statement. If you did not read the earlier chapters on individual rights and limited government (or if you are a socialist), you may disagree with her statement. But she is right.

There are countless examples of capitalism working: Hong Kong and South Korea are just two obvious ones. These are practical arguments, but they don't address the morality of capitalism. This chapter looks at the moral argument for capitalism.

As I said in the earlier chapters, for freedom to exist, individual rights must be the basis for all human interactions, and the role of government must be limited to the protection of individual rights. As Ayn Rand indicated above, capitalism is not merely practical. Capitalism is moral.

Capitalism allows for individual freedom. Freedom of trade between individuals is a critical characteristic of capitalism. If a proposed transaction is mutually beneficial, the transaction will be completed because both parties benefit. If the proposed transaction is not mutually beneficial, both parties may walk away. In a capitalist system, neither party is forced to be a sacrificial animal for the other party.

In non-capitalist systems (e.g., fascist, communist, socialist), if you are a productive person you will be forced (at gunpoint, if you resist) to give what you've earned to unproductive people. This is not considered charity in these systems. (I am in favor of some forms of charity.) In a non-capitalist system, some bureaucrat will determine what you "owe."

All non-capitalist economies are based on the collectivist/statist/socialist ideology. Collectivists, statists, and socialists speak of "community resources," "national resources," or "state resources." In other words, your productivity belongs to the collective, not to you. Individual rights are not possible in such a system. Everything you produce, and all your property, is subject to the whim of the collective. (It's more accurate to say "to the whim of the leaders of the collective.") These whims are easily converted into "legal" seizure. The old expression, "No working person is safe when Congress is in session," is appropriate in a socialist State.

Socialism's Fatal Flaw

The most influential non-capitalist, collectivistic political-economic system in the twenty-first century is socialism. Socialism has gained many advocates because it provides a "legal" way to acquire unearned wealth. Many decades of capitalism in Western industrialized countries have created great wealth. The socialists' intent is to re-distribute that wealth (wealth that they did not produce).

Socialism cannot work long-term. Living off the wealth of an earlier capitalist era will eventually end. Every civilized society must have producers. The concept of a "consumer society" is absurd. Great wealth, no matter how it's re-distributed, will eventually be totally consumed without further production.

Socialism provides no incentive for the highly productive. Why should you be highly productive when you know some bureaucrat can snatch away the product of your labor for the benefit of some loud, but unproductive, special-interest group?

Eventually, you'll see all the talented, innovative, highly productive people withdrawing from a socialist society. You can read *Atlas Shrugged* (Rand, 1957) to see a fictionalized, but possibly prophetic, depiction of this scenario.

Where communal ownership is the law, you quickly realize that you have no individual rights to life, liberty, property, or the pursuit of happiness. In a socialist society you are the servant of the collective, without individual rights.

Mixed Economy

The United States is still frequently called a capitalist society. It's not. The United States is a mixed economy. (By the time you read this, America may be a socialist economy.)

In the early twenty-first century, all Western democracies are either socialist or "mixed economies." A mixed economy is an attempt to blend capitalism (based on individual rights) with socialism (based on collective "rights"). If you read the earlier chapters, you know that collectives don't have rights, unless they have been usurped from individuals; thus, the blending of capitalism and socialism is immoral.

The mixed economy is believed to be a middle-of-the-road approach. It's not. Once capitalism has been forsaken, it's a slippery slope into socialism. Friedrich Hayek describes this process in his famous book, *The Road to Serfdom* (Hayek, 2007/1944).

The government in a mixed economy must eventually become a totalitarian regime to force any stubborn individualists to give up their individual rights. These "heavy-handed" regimes invariably claim to exert force for "the good of the majority." The earnings of productive people will be the target to finance the lifestyles of unproductive people and the State bureaucrats.

Capitalism and socialism are irreconcilable economic systems because they are based upon two irreconcilable philosophies. Capitalism is based on the philosophy of individualism; socialism is based on the philosophy of collectivism.

Capitalism is based on the exercising of the individual rights of free association and free trade; the free market decides who trades with whom. Socialism does not recognize individual rights, free association, free trade, or a free market. In a socialist state, a bureaucrat decides who trades with whom, under what state-determined regulations, and what prices will be paid.

The fatal flaw of a mixed economy is that it has no philosophical foundation. There are no consistent principles to answer political questions. Peikoff (1993, p.373) asks, "How is it to know when to respect individual rights and when to infringe them?"

In a mixed economy, decisions are based on feelings, emotions, whim, pressure groups, and majority vote. This leads to short-term irrational thinking. Quick fixes become the "solution" because no enduring principles direct the decision-making process. Guessing on a case-by-case basis leads to inconsistent case law and inconsistent government regulations. Society quickly degenerates into warring pressure groups using irrational, emotionally charged rhetoric to get their way.

Benefits of Capitalism

Capitalism, the only moral political-economic system, offers many benefits.

Obviously, capitalism creates great wealth. The examples are endless: the United States compared to Soviet Russia, West Germany compared to East Germany, South Korea compared to North Korea. Simply looking at Hong Kong should convince anybody that capitalism works.

Capitalism raises the standard of living for all its citizens, even the poorest of society. In a capitalist society every person who wants to work can find employment. The competent and highly motivated in a capitalist society generate amazing numbers of jobs. In contrast, very few jobs are created in a stifling socialist society. In a socialist society, the poor remain permanent dependents of the State.

Capitalism leads to a meritocracy. The more value you deliver in the form of products and services, the wealthier you become. If you are rewarded for creating value, you will create more value. In a socialist society, the fruits of your productivity are taken away by a bureaucrat and distributed to the unproductive members of the society. There is no incentive to be productive in a socialist State.

Capitalism relegates ethnicity and racism to a historical footnote. In a capitalist society, individuals are free to trade with whomever they want. You will trade with me if you benefit (profit) from the trade; if you benefit, you don't care what my ethnicity or race is. In a state-controlled socialist society, you may be forced to trade with me because the state has designated my group for special privileges; you must deal with me at no profit (or even a loss) to yourself; you will resent my group.

Finally, capitalism leads to self-esteem and self-reliance. A loss of "face" or self-esteem always leads to emotional and social problems. Frustration with self always leads to frustration with others. Capitalism requires self-reliance rather than dependency on the collective (the State). Welfare is a dehumanizing tool of a socialist State. Anybody who has transitioned from welfare to work will tell you that he or she feels liberated. Every adult needs the sense of self-reliance that comes only from the freedom offered by a capitalist system. Capitalism is the only system that supports individual rights and individual initiative.

Anti-Capitalists

Austrian economist Ludwig von Mises explained why so many people hate capitalism. Capitalism's rewards are based on merit. According to Mises, "if merit alone decides, then the unsuccessful feel themselves insulted and humiliated" (2006/1956, p.8). Unwilling to take responsibility for their own failure, these people look for a scapegoat. The scapegoat for the unsuccessful-unproductive is the successful-productive. This irrational evasion of reality leads to class warfare, invariably led by power-seeking socialist politicians.

Capitalism offers freedom, but it also requires self-responsibility. Unfortunately, many people reject self-responsibility. Clearly, the unsuccessful do not want to blame themselves for their own failure in a free society. "They are socialists because they are blinded by envy and ignorance" (Mises, 2006/1956, p.28).

Mises (2006/1956) said, "No intelligent man could fail to recognize that what the socialists, communists, and [State] planners were aiming at was the most radical abolition of the individuals' freedom and the establishment of government omnipotence" (p.57). Unfortunately, people "blinded by envy and ignorance" are not thinking intelligently.

Conclusion

To whom Mises called the "intelligent," it should seem obvious that individual rights, limited government, and capitalism are moral and practical necessities for individuals to live free and to prosper. But be aware; there will always be socialist forces attempting to eliminate your individual rights, to expand government, and to abolish capitalism.

In the following chapters, I will show you how two warring philosophies have existed throughout history. The anti-freedom forces of collectivism/statism/socialism are supported by power-seeking politicians and the majority of people (the unproductive). Make no mistake, if you are a successful, productive, freedom-seeking individual, you are in the minority. Fortunately, the forces of individualism/ libertarianism/capitalism have morality and rationality on their side. But the majority of people (the jealous and unproductive) are always willing to be immoral and irrational to get what they want.

In Chapter 5, *A Brief History of Political Philosophy*, you will see the battle of statism-versus-libertarianism going all the way back to Plato and Aristotle. In Chapter 6, *A Brief History of Economics*, you'll see the same philosophical battle called socialism-versus-capitalism.

In the next chapter, we will look at the importance of rational thinking. Rational thinking leads to individualism, libertarianism, and capitalism. Irrational thinking leads to collectivism, statism, and socialism.

References ————————————————

Hayek, Friedrich (2007/1944). *The Road to Serfdom*. (Edited by Bruce Caldwell.) Chicago: University of Chicago Press.

Mises, Ludwig von (2006/1956). *The Anti-Capitalist Mentality*. Indianapolis, IN: Liberty Fund.

Peikoff, Leonard. (1993). *Objectivism*. New York: Meridian.

Rand, Ayn. (1957). *Atlas Shrugged*. New York: Signet.

Rand, Ayn. (1967). *Capitalism: The Unknown Ideal*. New York: Signet.

Chapter 4

Rational Thinking

THROUGHOUT THE FIRST three chapters of this book, I have expressed my advocacy for individual rights, limited government, and capitalism as the basis for moral behavior. These three recommendations are not independent of each other. You can't adopt one without the others.

While I'm an advocate of all three, and welcome invitations to speak on any one of them, I insist that the deeper and more critical issue is a philosophical one. The most important message I can share in this book is the importance of thinking rationally. (If you think irrationally, your decisions may work short-term, but they will always lead to disaster long-term.)

We live in a rational world. During eras of rational thinking, we discover truths that allow us to do away with myths in the physical sciences and social sciences. During eras of irrational thinking, societies fall back into mysticism and darkness.

We live in a period when rational thinking and irrational thinking are trying to co-exist. The problem: rational thinking and irrational thinking cannot co-exist. You can have one or the other, but not both. Irrational thinking always displaces rational thinking because irrational thinking requires less effort; thus, irrational thinking is practiced by the masses. Irrational thinking allows individuals (and entire societies) to ignore reality and live in fantasy. This works for a short period of time. Eventually, however, reality comes crashing back into the fantasy. "Harsh" reality will demand attention from the people who are least prepared to deal with it, so, like children unprepared to deal with adult decisions, an authority figure is sought for guidance. A dictator, who promises to have all the answers, inevitably emerges.

In the early twenty-first century, rational thinking is becoming a rarity. While a remnant of rational thinking continues, contributing great technological and scientific advances, irrational thinking increasingly dominates social, political, and economic debates.

Irrational thinking leads a society into disaster because, in actuality, irrational thinking is not thinking at all. Irrational thinking is based upon whim and emotion. Irrational thinking is irresponsible because it abandons the basic principles of reality. We don't live in a world where reality can be ignored for long.

Let's look at what has led us to irrational thinking en masse. Let's start by asking, "How do we know what is true?"

Theories of Truth

In philosophy there are two theories of truth: the correspondence theory of truth and the coherence theory of truth. This is not simply a tiresome academic distinction; there are serious implications here for our actions in the real world.

The *correspondence theory* of truth states that something can only be true if the theorist can show how the theory or concept corresponds to the real world. This is an Aristotelian approach to truth. Aristotle disagreed with his mentor, Plato, on this concept. Plato believed there was another higher realm where theories, concepts, and ideas exist separately from physical reality. Aristotle insisted that concepts and theories must correspond with physical reality.

The *coherence theory* of truth states that something is true if it is internally consistent (coherent). In other words, if an argument can be made for a theory, concept, idea, or philosophical system with no inconsistencies, it must be true; it does not have to correspond to anything in the known world. This thinking is clearly Platonic. It creates a theoretical dimension where unchallengeable ideas exist. Advocates of this theory of truth believe a realm of theory exists without any correspondence to the world in which we live.

When I first heard about the coherence theory of truth, I started laughing. I could imagine this primitive way of thinking existing in pre-Socratic times or the Dark Ages. But I was shocked to find out that the coherence theory of truth dominates western culture in the twenty-first century. As a believer in the correspondence theory of truth, I suddenly realized that I was a member of a small minority.

In the twenty-first century most people still believe theory (and ideas) can stand alone without corresponding to the real world. This belief is not limited to mystics or to the fringe of society. This belief that "theory can be valid separate from the real world" is pervasive.

I was especially surprised to find this belief in the business world, where I have worked as both an executive and a consultant for most of my life. I constantly heard comments such as, "That's fine in theory, but it's not true in practice."

I wasn't too surprised to find the coherence theory in the academic world, where theory is considered all-important, and practice is seen as the lowly activity of the bourgeoisie. The real world is seen as too plebeian to concern most academics in their ivory towers.

Perhaps the most dramatic display I've seen of belief in two separate worlds (practice and theory) happened during one of my evening MBA classes several years ago. Keep in mind, evening MBA students are typically mid-level managers in the business world.

I had just quoted Kurt Lewin, who said, "There's nothing more practical than a good theory." I then casually added, "I am sure you'll agree with Lewin. What makes a theory good is the fact that it's practical." After a brief pause, the room exploded into disagreement. I heard a host of objections, but these three seemed to be the most widely shared:

- "Theory has nothing to do with practice!"
- "There's no such thing as a practical theory; theory is not practical."
- "Theory has no place in the real world, even a good theory."

I am rarely at a loss for words, but I was speechless. I called for a 15-minute break. During the break I talked with a few students about their reactions. Clearly, they were adherents of the coherence theory of truth (even though they did not use that term).

After the break, I asked my students how they made management decisions without a philosophical system with clear principles to refer to. With a look of bewilderment they said, "In management we make decisions on a case-by-case basis." After a reflective pause, I asked, "But how do you maintain consistency in your decisions if you use a knee-jerk emotional reaction for each decision?" Their response: blank stares.

While you should have a rational philosophical system to make consistently effective decisions, clearly it's not the basis for most people's decision making.

In the next section, let's look at the popular philosophical systems in America today.

Flawed American Philosophies

The dominant and pervasive philosophies in America in the early twenty-first century are pragmatism and utilitarianism.

Pragmatism

For most of my life I considered myself to be a pragmatist. One day I realized that saying I was a pragmatist was an admission that I had no philosophical basis for my decisions at all. I was making decisions based on whim, not principles.

Most pragmatists claim to be using "good ole common sense." But, since this "common sense" doesn't involve principles or rigorous rational thinking, how do pragmatists make decisions? These pragmatists say "whatever works is true."

But in a world where consequences do not follow immediately after decisions, how do you know what *works*? Can you see problems with this philosophy? Evaluate this: All people need health care, and all people need food and shelter; therefore, the government should be responsible for health care, as well as food and shelter for everyone. The government can provide for everyone's every need—temporarily. But this approach is clearly not rational. The government will quickly go broke. This thinking considers short-term benefits but ignores long-term consequences. You need enduring principles.

Pragmatism has dominated American thinking for more than a century. The writings of William James (America's leading pragmatist) go completely unchallenged in most areas of American life.

In American politics, pragmatic decisions are made without any discussion of principles. In the absence of principles, people decide based on emotion, whim, or current popularity. These decisions, at best, result in a short-term fix; at worst, these decisions exacerbate the real problem and create more and bigger problems.

Pragmatists claim to look for best-of-both-world solutions. The problem with this noble-sounding quest is that it often ignores reality. In reality, many of these "worlds" cannot co-exist. Without guiding philosophical principles, the mindless brute force of "majority-rules" is invoked. Truth cannot be determined by democratic vote.

You may now be asking, "What's wrong with a majority-rules society?" Well, the unintended consequences are deeply disturbing. Even though the consequences of majority-rules decision making are not discussed in America, it's worth your time to think them through. Clearly, individual rights are constantly at risk, unless you are always in the majority.

Utilitarianism

Majority-rule decision making is justified by "utilitarianism." Utilitarians believe social, political, and economic decisions should be based on one criterion: How will the most people benefit? This concept of maximizing "utility" is a simplistic process of counting the number of people who benefit. Bluntly stated, the majority benefits, while the minority suffers any negative consequences. There is no need to discuss principles; utilitarians simply ask for a "show of hands" (the majority rules).

In a utilitarian society, the ends justify the means. Since the majority can always out-vote the minority, the minority is always subjected to abuse. The minorities (the highly productive, the wealthy, and non-conformists) live in fear of abuse. Individual rights are usurped by the collective. What has been earned by the minority can be taken away at the whim of the majority.

There are different forms of utilitarianism, of course. John Stuart Mill in his book *Utilitarianism* expressed his concern about a strictly popular vote. He believed a distinction must be made between the lower pleasures and the higher pleasures. My question is, "Who will decide what is a 'lower pleasure' and what is a 'higher pleasure'?" The answer, you guessed it—a bureaucrat. Again, your individual rights will be sacrificed for the "good of the people."

Another form of utilitarianism madness is negative utilitarianism. Advocates of negative utilitarianism (NU) believe we must make decisions that will eliminate the most human suffering (instead of promoting the most human pleasure). It has been suggested that NU will complete its purpose when it determines the quickest and least painful method of killing all of humanity! I don't think I need to state the obvious flaws in this philosophy.

The Need for Rational Thinking

While I am critical of almost all of the philosophical systems taught in university philosophy courses today, I believe a rational view of existence (a philosophy) is critical to human happiness.

An animal has no need for a philosophical system. It lives on a level of basic survival. Its limited cognitive capabilities prevent it from asking the questions that philosophy attempts to answer.

Human beings need a philosophy. Even a career limited to only physical labor is not devoid of philosophical questions. At the end of a long day of physical labor, philosophical questions inevitably rise to the surface of consciousness. Human beings cannot ignore these questions with impunity. We are not like animals; we cannot live as if we were mindless.

The academics divide the study of philosophy into five fields:

1. metaphysics—the study of the nature of the universe (What exists?)

2. epistemology—the study of human knowledge (What can we know?)

3. ethics—the study of values (What is right and wrong?)

4. politics—the study of social systems and government (How should people relate to one other?)

5. esthetics—the study of art (What is beautiful?)

Leonard Peikoff has stated, "For a philosophical idea to function properly as a guide, one must know the full system to which it belongs" (Peikoff, 1991, p.3). Throughout this book, I have spoken about my philosophical system of rational individualism. To live (and thrive) as a rational individualist, you do not have to agree with everything in my system, but you should strive to develop a philosophical system that you can clearly articulate to yourself (and to other rational beings). Let me share with you what I consider to be essential for rational individualism.

Metaphysically speaking, existence exists. The reality that you perceive through your five senses is real. There is no evil genie or demon trying to trick you. It is a waste of money to support scientific research if you believe the physical world around you is an unknowable illusion.

Epistemologically speaking, existence is knowable. This may sound overly simplistic and obvious, but it is not widely accepted in the ivory towers of academia or on the streets of America.

We live on a planet in an apparently infinite universe. While awe-inspiring, the universe is knowable. The vastness and complexity of the universe is not beyond human comprehension. In the early twenty-first century, we have already mapped the human genome (the sequences of the three-billion chemical-based pairs that make up human DNA) and explored deep space with our technology. While this knowledge will not impress anybody living in the twenty-fifth century, we fortunately don't live in the darkness of our ancestors. Centuries of ignorance are yielding to scientific proof that the world in which we live is rational.

Of course, human beings continue to act irrationally. But they act in a rational universe. We now know that hurricanes, earthquakes, and solar eclipses are not "acts of God," but the results of cause-and-effect rational relationships.

Irrational thinking has not been limited to mystics and witch doctors. Academic philosophers have also abandoned rational thinking to live in worlds of their own making. Using the coherence theory of truth (explained earlier), these academics have pursued their abstractions into intellectual cul-de-sacs. They proudly proclaim that, based on their theories, existence doesn't exist. Needless to say, they have been discarded by society as irrelevant, and have become laughingstocks for school children who know better.

Human beings have a natural ability to imagine what does not exist. That's good. That's part of the creative process. However, imagination can lead to irrational and nonsensical thinking if it's not subjected to rigorous reality-checks. Our theories, concepts, and ideas must submit to reality, not the other way around.

While questions about the supernatural and the unknowable (e.g., What existed before the universe began?) can make for interesting discussion, they should not lead to hateful arguments and wars. We owe it to our fellow human beings to be respectful of their religious faith. It's impossible to "win" a hateful argument.

Equally disgraceful is the assertion that our perceptions determine reality. Remember what I said earlier, "Our theories, concepts, and ideas must submit to reality, not the other way around." Only childish fantasy asserts, "I believe it, therefore it is true."

Holding on to an irrational belief doesn't make the object of the belief real, but the consequences of the irrational belief are real. Believing that Santa Claus will pay off your credit card debts, or that Superman will lift your tractor out of the ditch, will lead to the very real consequence of bankruptcy. Believing won't make it so.

Reality exists independent of our perceptions, wishes, and irrational theories. Attempts to evade the real world lead to an increasingly irrational mind. Since it's the rational mind that separates us from the animals, nothing is more self-destructive than irrational thinking. Reality is not subordinated to our thinking; our thinking must be subordinated to reality.

Conclusion

Can you see the fate of all those who reject rational thinking? Thinking irrationally leads individuals and societies to disaster.

Rational thinking is grounded in (corresponds with) reality. Once you see the rational necessity of individual rights, political-economic decisions are easier to make. Once you understand that human survival (and thriving) rationally requires individual rights, you understand that limited government and capitalism are essential, not optional.

Irrational thinking requires the rejection of reality in favor of fantasy. The irrational thinker says, "I want it, therefore it is." Irrational thinking makes life easier short-term, but ultimately makes it much harder. Irrational thinking leads to ever-increasing complexity in decision-making, in an effort to continue avoiding reality. Irrational thinking's short-term "benefits" do not justify the long-term painful consequences it causes.

Rational thinking requires the rejection of fantasy. Rational thinking does not make life easy, but it makes life easier to deal with.

It is critical that you be always cognizant of the philosophical differences between individualism and collectivism, libertarianism and statism, capitalism and socialism, as well as

rational thinking and irrational thinking. The following table
serves as a quick reference guide:

Individualism	Collectivism
Libertarianism	Statism
Capitalism	Socialism
Rational	Anti-rational
Individual Rights	"Group Rights"
Individual Freedom	Government Control
Private Property	Public Property
Productive People	Unproductive People
Seeking Freedom	Seeking Power
Empirical	Anti-Empirical
Correspondence Theory of Truth	Coherence Theory of Truth
Reality-Based	Wish-Based
Real World	Utopian

TABLE 4.1 *The Competing Philosophies*

References

Peikoff, Leonard. (1991). *Objectivism*. New York: Meridian.

CHAPTER 5

A Brief History of Political Philosophy

IN ORDER TO MAKE political decisions rationally, you must understand your own political philosophy. You must know whether you are a libertarian or a statist. Unfortunately, few people devote the time and effort to a critical review of political philosophy. This lack of effort is embarrassingly obvious when listening to American political candidates. They say they support contradictory beliefs with great sincerity—and great ignorance.

You can avoid looking like a clueless American politician by reading the material in this chapter and then pursuing your own study of political philosophy. The study of political philosophy is actually very intellectually stimulating. (Please forget any bad experiences you had in a university "Introduction to Philosophy" or "Political Science" course.)

The roots of western political philosophies can be traced to two ancient philosophical systems: Plato's or Aristotle's. More than two thousand years ago these two thinkers wrestled with the same political issues that we wrestle with today. Plato was Aristotle's mentor. They shared the same questions but rarely the same answers. As I briefly discuss each man's system, you will see the connections to modern politics.

After successfully defending itself against Darius and Xerxes, the kings of Persia, the Greek city-state of Athens (with the help of Sparta) enjoyed a period of peace, security, and prosperity. It was during this period that western philosophy was born. The port of Athens became a busy market for the exchange of ideas, as well as products. The Athenians were exposed to hundreds of religions and philosophies. Obviously, all of these systems could not be right. Thus, the Athenians became skeptical and turned to natural science and reason for explanations about the world.

Plato

Plato (427-347BC) had an extraordinary teacher and mentor, Socrates (470-399BC). Socrates had all kinds of students (aristocrats, socialists, and anarchists). He forced all of them to do one thing: think. Socrates would not accept platitudes and meaningless words. Socrates would not have approved of America's current political candidates.

Plato was born into an aristocratic Athenian family. He excelled as a soldier and was a champion athlete. He was known for his broad shoulders; he was not what you'd picture as an idealist philosopher.

Socrates cultivated a love of learning in Plato. Socrates taught Plato the importance of careful analysis and rational discussion. When Socrates died in 399BC, Plato said, "I thank God I was born in the age of Socrates."

Plato hated democracy. He detested the stupidity of the mob. The Peloponnesian War, between Athens and Sparta, began three years before Plato's birth (430BC) and did not end until Plato was 27 years old (400BC). Athens was defeated by the rival Greek city-state of Sparta.

Athens had been a democracy (even though more than half of the inhabitants were slaves). Many Athenians, including Plato, believed democracy made Athens too weak to fight Sparta. Plato made it clear that his intention was to destroy democracy and replace it with a ruling class.

After Socrates' death, Plato wandered the world for twelve years. No doubt what he saw on these adventures influenced the writing of *The Republic* (Plato's utopian state).

At the age of 40, Plato returned to Athens (387BC). He had become knowledgeable in philosophy, poetry, science, and art.

The Republic

Plato's most important work, at least for the purpose of this book, is *The Republic*. Virtually every German philosopher (from Kant to Hegel to Marx to Nietzsche) borrowed from Plato's utopian state. In *The Republic* you find socialism, communism, eugenics, master versus slave morality, the sacrifice of individual rights to the state, and the justification for a ruling elite.

Plato criticized various forms of government from aristocracy to democracy. He was especially hard on democracy. He believed a democracy ruins itself by allowing uneducated people to elect political leaders. Plato's criticism is insightful, but his solution is terrifying to anyone who believes in individual rights and limited government. Libertarians are understandably horrified by Plato's statist solutions.

Plato believed an all-powerful State was necessary to keep people safe. Individual liberties must be sacrificed to the State for the purpose of security.

Strict eugenic supervision was critical to Plato's vision. No man or woman could mate who was not in perfect health. Health certificates were required of brides and grooms. Babies born of unlicensed mating, as well as those born deformed, were left to die. Brave and "better" males were given a variety of mates, based on the assumption that "better" males fathered "better" sons.

Children in Plato's "It Takes a Village" communist society belonged to the State. All boys were called brother, all girls were called sister, older men were called father, and older women were called mother.

Children learned that they were not individuals, but that they belonged to the collective. Children owed "obligations" to the State, which granted the privilege to live.

At the age of ten, all children were taken from their parents by the State. Plato believed any damage done by the parents could still be reversed at that age. Plato would have approved of Hitler's youth camps.

Plato believed children must receive rigorous training in sports and gymnastics. He believed this would eliminate the need for all medicines and physicians. Plato said Utopia cannot afford unhealthy people and invalids. The State must be built on strong bodies.

Plato's utopia offered full equality of educational opportunity (universal education). Boys and girls of every social rank tried themselves at science, art, and every type of knowledge and skill. Plato believed society would benefit as the individual's innate talents were revealed. This is one place where I actually agree with Plato.

This first-phase of education would continue until the age of 20. Then the first round of elimination exams was administered. Students who failed would go to work in factories, businesses, or on farms.

Those students who passed received ten more years of education before facing a second round of elimination exams at age 30. Those who failed this round of exams became executive assistants and military officers.

The students who passed the second elimination round received five years of philosophical training. Here the students studied Plato's "Realm of the Forms"; they learned about Universals and Idealism.

At the age of 35, the "academic" education of the elite was complete. Now they must earn a living, by the sweat of their brow, alongside businessmen and factory workers. At age 50, they automatically became rulers of the State (if they survived).

Plato is willing to stoop to the lowest forms of manipulation to implement his socialist vision. In order to get everyone to comply, he invents a supernatural authority: God. Not a force or impersonal power, but a living God who can stir fear and self-sacrifice. The individual must know that he/she is not arguing with Plato or the State about his/her "station in life," but is arguing with God Himself. Of course, rewards in the afterlife are offered to those who submit.

Plato's communist State had central planning. Trade and production was regulated to prevent "excess individual wealth."

The excess, defined by Plato as four times the possessions of average citizens, was "returned" to the State. The regulators directed all economic activity and determine who should do which job.

All ethical decisions in Plato's utopia were based upon what is best for the collective, the State. Individual sovereignty must be sacrificed to the State; the welfare of the collective was supreme.

Criticism of Plato

Needless to say, as an individualist, libertarian, and capitalist, I am appalled by Plato's socialist State. I believe the sacrifice of the individual to the State is immoral.

I do commend Plato for his insight into the innate talents of individuals. Plato correctly observed the silliness of the blank-slate doctrine. (Unfortunately, that is beyond the scope of this book.)

Plato's belief in educating women is also commendable. Every human being deserves an equal opportunity. But rewards in the society should be based on merit.

Plato's Influence

Plato's influence in the West (as well as his indirect influence in Asia) is immeasurable. All utopian statist visions are children of Plato's thought. The German philosophers, Kant, Hegel, and Marx, all envisioned individuals with a single purpose: to serve the collective. The individual has no rights, just duties.

Aristotle

Aristotle (384-322BC) was Plato's most brilliant student. But Aristotle did not build upon the work of his mentor; he developed his own school of thought. It's hard to imagine a student disagreeing more with his teacher, even though they seemed to share a mutual admiration.

Aristotle was a Macedonian. He was born in Stagira, 200 miles north of Athens. At the time, the Greeks considered the Macedonians to be barbarians. Aristotle's father was the physician to the King of Macedon, Amyntas (the grandfather of Alexander the Great).

The exact year Aristotle was sent to Athens to study under Plato is debatable, but historians agree on a long period of study ranging to as many as 20 years. Plato was more than 40 years older than Aristotle, so it's unlikely that they ever had a peer relationship.

While studying under Plato, Aristotle spent great sums of money to build an extensive collection of books. His library of handwritten manuscripts covered a wide range of subjects. This, no doubt, led to Aristotle's interest in classifying knowledge (one of his great contributions to Western thought).

In 343BC, King Philip of Macedon (son of Amyntas) invited Aristotle to become the educator of his son, Alexander. Alexander was 13; Aristotle was 41. These two Macedonians would reshape the political and intellectual worlds. Alexander the Great conquered the entire known world. Aristotle ruled the intellectual world for the next 2,000 years.

In 338BC, Philip (Alexander's father) defeated Athens and united the independent city-states of Greece (with chains). When Philip was assassinated, Alexander took the throne. The Athenians associated Aristotle with the hated "Macedonian party."

Aristotle's Prolific Work

Aristotle was 53 years old when he opened his school, the Lyceum. The Lyceum had plenty of students and was well funded. With Alexander the Great, the Ruler of the World, as a patron, The Lyceum had everything imaginable. At any one time, Alexander had a thousand men gathering zoological and botanical material throughout the known world for Aristotle's school. Aristotle had an army of researchers, scribes, and assistants at his disposal.

Whereas Plato's Academy focused on abstract mathematics and political philosophy, Aristotle's Lyceum studied the natural sciences as well as philosophy.

In addition to eating meals with the Master, Aristotle's students would have discussions with him while they walked along the Peripatos. This method of teaching on the walking path, the Peripatos, became a defining characteristic of the school. The Lyceum became known as the Peripatetic School.

Aristotle's written work during this time cannot be properly expressed with the word "prolific." His work is estimated to fill 400 to 1,000 volumes: physical science, ethics, politics, metaphysics, and esthetics. He developed the discipline of logic (methods for testing and correcting thought). We also know that he wrote literary dialogues (considered to be comparable to Plato's); unfortunately, these have been lost.

Aristotle built the terminology and methodology used in science and philosophy to this day. He was known as "The Philosopher" for the next two thousand years.

Universals

The debate over "universals," begun by Plato and Aristotle continues to this day. Plato taught that the universal (the concept of "man," "king," or "tree") is more important than any individual man, king, or tree. According to Plato, only the universal matters; only the universal is lasting. To Plato, the individual is nothing more than an unimportant wave in a constant surf.

Plato's belief is obvious in *The Republic*, where the individual is only a cog in the collective machine.

The absurd anti-individual implications of Plato's thought are epitomized in the German philosophers. Kant, Hegel, and Marx saw the individual as existing only to serve the will of the collective or the State. Plato was the first of this line of statist political philosophers.

Aristotle taught that universals exist only as a convenient abstraction in thought. A universal is only a concept. A universal is a nomina (a name) for the members of a class or category. According to Aristotle's followers, the Nominalists, the class or category itself does not exist in reality. They believe it's only the individual that matters.

Aristotle believed we live in a world of individual and specific objects. He saw Plato's thinking as mystical and other-worldly. Aristotle believed truth must correspond to objective reality. His thinking is still very influential two thousand years later in Ayn Rand's philosophy of Objectivism.

Aristotle's "Golden Mean"

In Raphael's famous painting, *The School at Athens*, Plato and Aristotle are walking through The Academy in obvious disagreement. The utopian Plato is gesturing toward the heavens, as if truth resides in a higher realm. Aristotle has his hand at belt height to indicate the "Golden Mean."

It is important to note, Aristotle is not pointing at the ground (as some commentators have said). Aristotle sought truth between the extremes. He disapproved of Plato's utopian other-worldliness, but he would have been equally appalled by the down-and-dirty unethical politics of Machiavelli.

Aristotle believed Plato's communist state was a utopian solution to the problems of society. He was horrified by

Plato's suggestions to abolish the family and to abolish private property. Aristotle correctly believed Plato's State would destroy the benefits of individual initiative and innovation. Aristotle believed individual liberty, privacy, and property rights must not be sacrificed to the State.

Aristotle wanted a strong government, but not the one envisioned by Plato. Like Plato, he saw what happened to the weak and inept Athenian democracy. He sought a Golden Mean in politics: a constitutional government, a mean between democracy and aristocracy. Aristotle believed an aristocratic class of educated and informed individuals must form the pool of political candidates. While an aristocratic ruling class may be unattractive to twenty-first century Americans, it's become painfully obvious that American political candidates are not the best and brightest.

Plato vs. Aristotle

Friedrich Schlegel once said, "Every man is born either a Platonist or an Aristotelian." While that is apparently true for most people, I believe it is intellectually lazy to accept either school of thought wholeheartedly without rigorous study.

For the most part, I am an Aristotelian. I am proud to be associated with the Aristotelian intellectual tradition of individualism, limited government, and libertarianism. The followers of this tradition include John Locke, Adam Smith, the Enlightenment thinkers, the American Founding Fathers, the free-market economists, and Ayn Rand. These Aristotelians have bravely stood up against collectivism, big government, and socialist ideologues.

Aristotle rejected Plato's communism and argued for individual property rights. Aristotle said, "What is common to many is taken least care of, for all men have greater regard for what is their own than for what they possess in common with others."

However, there are problems with Aristotle's philosophy. Aristotle's views about women are shameful. He is often defended by his followers who say women were not typically educated at the time, so he had no way of knowing what they were capable of doing intellectually. That's unacceptable.

Plato believed girls and boys should both be educated. Plato believed in a meritocracy; the individual should be limited only by his or her ability. On these two things, Plato was right, Aristotle was wrong.

While Aristotle is rightfully considered by many to be one of the fathers of libertarianism, all of his philosophy should not be adopted without critique.

Statism vs. Libertarianism

Plato and Aristotle fired the first volleys in the war between statism and libertarianism. Every political philosopher ever since has wrestled with these issues.

Statist political philosophers typically call themselves "Rationalists," and follow the Platonic epistemological (the study of how we know what we know) tradition. They believe knowledge and truth can be arrived at apriori (without experience). The term "rationalism" as it's used here is a misnomer. Rationalists are not rational.

These Platonic "rationalists" believe in the coherence theory of truth; something is true if the argument has no internal inconsistencies. They feel there is no need to reconcile their arguments with the real world. If their theory disagrees with the world, the world is wrong. This, in my mind, should be called "irrationalism."

Over the entrance to Plato's Academy was a sign that read "Let No Man Ignorant of Geometry Enter Here." This devout faith in higher abstractions, while ignoring physical reality, still exists in early twenty-first century philosophy and science. Physicists known as string theorists say that there are six, seven, or even eleven dimensions. These physicists insist it's true because they have the mathematics to prove it. If you are reading this book in a room with more than three dimensions, you are in a mental institution. (I am glad to know my book is penetrating unexpected markets.)

Libertarian political philosophers typically call themselves "empiricists," and follow the Aristotelian epistemological tradition. They believe knowledge and truth can be arrived at only through experience.

These Aristotelian empiricists believe in the correspondence theory of truth; something is true if it corresponds to the real world, which we experience through our five senses. If their theory disagrees with the world, they believe their theory is wrong.

As we will see throughout the remainder of this chapter, most political philosophers are either Platonic or Aristotelian when it comes to the rationalism-empiricism epistemological debate. It greatly affects whether you'll be a statist or libertarian. You will see that the British, Scottish, and American thinkers are empiricists; the Continentals (including the French, Italians, and Germans) are rationalists. The implications are dramatic.

John Locke

Libertarianism (as we know it today) was born in Holland and England during the seventeenth century. While Aristotle contributed to libertarian thinking, John Locke (1632-1704) must be considered to be the Father of Libertarianism. Locke was a political philosopher ideally suited for his age in England.

In France, the Bourbon kings (Louis XIII and Louis XIV) had ruled for nearly 100 years. They claimed they ruled by divine right. In England, such claims were unacceptable.

In England, Protestant plotters made plans to rid themselves of the despotic Catholic King James II (1633-1701). John Locke was closely associated with the Protestant rebels, so he fled to Holland in 1683. At that time, Holland was a liberal country where freethinkers and religious dissenters from all over Europe resided.

Over the next five years in Holland, Locke concentrated on his two most important works, *Essay Concerning Human Understanding* and *Two Treatises of Government*. Meanwhile back home, the English Parliament rid England of James II and offered the English throne (in the form of joint sovereignty) to the Dutch Protestant William III of Orange (1650-1702) and his English wife Mary II (daughter of James II).

In 1688, John Locke sailed to England with William and Mary (along with 15,000 troops). For multiple reasons this became known as the "Glorious Revolution." It was glorious in that it was bloodless. It was also glorious because it led to reforms that made England the freest country in Europe. The sovereignty of parliament was established. A bill of rights became law. The Toleration Act (1689) allowed religious factions to worship as they saw fit; this meant the Church of England lost its monopoly power over religion and education. Freedom of the press soon followed.

In *Two Treatises of Government*, Locke argued against the divine right of kings and spoke boldly about individual freedom and natural rights. Locke's ideas became a critical part of the U.S. Constitution. Americans owe a debt to Locke.

Locke believed the consent of the people was the basis of government's authority. The government has no other duties beyond protecting the life, liberty, and property of its individual citizens. Locke believed the government's purpose was to serve the individual, not the other way around.

Locke clearly states that the people are justified in rebelling against the government if the government uses power in an arbitrary way without the consent of the people. In *Two Treatises*, Locke justifies the Whig rebellion and revolution of 1688, which led to the coronation of William and Mary, and denounces the Jacobite rebellion against William and Mary in 1689.

For Locke the most important rights are property rights. From a Lockean viewpoint, you cannot have other rights (life, liberty, free speech, etc.) if your property rights are not protected. For example, if the government can take your property if you say something that's "politically incorrect," all of your rights are in jeopardy.

Locke was the first in a line of political philosophers who said neither the Church nor the State had first claim on your life, liberty, and property. These inalienable rights reside in you—the individual.

Locke's work was followed by the French Enlightenment, the Scottish Enlightenment, the American Founding Fathers and American Revolution, the French Revolution, and the Counter-Enlightenment.

The French Enlightenment

Locke's work was translated into French in 1701. The salons and coffee houses of Paris buzzed with talk about liberty. Locke's ideas consumed the intelligentsia.

In Paris the philosopher-novelist was the rage. By the end of Voltaire's life he was treated like a rock star. Voltaire's sharp tongue angered the ruling elite, but he was adored by everyone else.

Montesquieu (1689-1755) became one of the leaders of a group of intellectuals known as "the Philosophes" in Paris. The Philosophes were intellectuals, but not ivory-tower academics. It became stylish to read the Philosophes.

In 1721, Montesquieu published *The Persian Letters*, an anti-establishment novel in the form of a series of letters written by two Persians, Usbek and Ricca, who describe the absurd things they saw in France. The novel was the century's best-seller until Voltaire published *Candide* in 1759.

Voltaire (1694-1778) was the most outspoken of the French Enlightenment writers. His uncontrolled wit landed him in the Bastille more than once. While exiled in England, Voltaire wrote one of his most influential books, *Letters Concerning the English Nation*. Voltaire spoke of England's religious tolerance, liberalism in politics and commerce, and vigor in science and philosophy. Many believe when Voltaire's *Letters* arrived in France, it was the beginning of the end for France's Ancien Régime.

Denis Diderot (1713-1784) was another leader of the Philosophes. Diderot was the organizing force behind the writing of the Encyclopédie, to which many of the Philosophes contributed.

The Encyclopédie describes a Philosophe as "One who, trampling on prejudice, tradition, universal consent, authority—in a word, all that enslaves most minds—dares to think for himself, to go back and search for the clearest general principles, to admit nothing except on the testimony of his experience and his reason" (Spencer & Krauze, 2006, p.51).

The leading salons of Paris vied to get the Philosophes to join them. The purpose of the salons was to stimulate intellectual discussion of the issues of the day. The salons were held in the homes of wealthy aristocratic women. These women served as hosts and actively participated in the discussions. Diderot said the gentlemen's comments were very entertaining because they were typically trying to impress the ladies.

There were some remarkable women at this time in Paris. Mme. d'Epinay wrote articles on philosophy, politics, and economics, in addition to theater and book reviews. She recorded many of the ideas, theories, and comments offered during the meetings of the Philosophes.

Mme. du Châtelet, Voltaire's companion, translated Isaac Newton's work into French. In addition to collaborating with Voltaire, she wrote independently on scientific topics. She also published a book on Christian Wolff's interpretation of Leibniz's philosophy.

It's interesting to note Diderot's attack on the traditional French distinction between liberal and mechanical arts. The French were interested in a liberal education in the classics only for the elite; they looked down their noses at the mechanical "arts." Diderot, the son of a master cutler, said, "How strangely we judge! We demand that people should be usefully engaged, and we disdain useful men" (Spencer & Krauze, 2006, p.65). Diderot contributed countless entries to the Encyclopédie about the crafts and trades based upon the interviews he did with tradesmen and craftsmen throughout France.

Finally, the influence of Montesquieu's *Spirit of the Laws* (1748) should not be underestimated. *Spirit of the Laws* is a great sociological work as well as a political treatise. Montesquieu was attempting to explain why governments were the way they were.

The book concludes that parliaments must limit the power of the king. Montesquieu's timing could not have been better; the book was an immediate best-seller.

Montesquieu's belief in individual liberty had an incalculably great influence on the Scottish Enlightenment thinkers and the American Founding Fathers.

The Scottish Enlightenment

The Scottish Enlightenment had a different flavor than the French Enlightenment. It was a boys-only debate in Scotland. This was a time of great advances in industrial technology and engineering throughout Great Britain. The highly practical Scots had no time for poetry. The Scots wanted ideas that could be tested in the "real" world. Not surprisingly, the Scots focused on economics and political philosophy and devoted less time to metaphysics and epistemology.

David Hume (1711-1776) set the tone for the Scottish Enlightenment. Hume took Locke's empirical (knowledge through experience only) approach. Hume believed all knowledge, even ethics, must be found through fact and observation.

Adam Smith (1723-1790), a close friend of Hume, is best known for *The Wealth of Nations* (1776). While *Wealth of Nations* established Adam Smith as the Father of Economics, he thought of himself as a philosopher. Smith taught at the University of Glasgow, first as a professor of logic and then as a professor of moral philosophy (ethics). Although lesser known today, Smith's *Theory of Moral Sentiments* was very influential as well.

I'll have more to say about the Scots in general and Adam Smith in particular in Chapter 6, *A Brief History of Economics*.

American Founding Fathers

The American Founding Fathers (including Franklin, Adams, Paine, Jefferson, and Washington) all read Locke and the Enlightenment thinkers. All of them believed strongly in the individual rights of life, liberty, and property.

Benjamin Franklin (1706-1790) was the eldest and in many ways the most influential of the Founding Fathers. "Franklin was known in the Paris salons as a true philosophe and scientist" (Spencer & Krauze, 2006, p.144). Franklin started publishing his *Poor Richard's Almanac* (a self-help journal) in 1732. His ideas continued to be sought for the next 60 years.

John Adams (1735-1826) was a tireless contributor to American liberty. Adams served as a diplomat to France and Holland during the Revolutionary War. He served as vice president for two terms under Washington, and then served as America's second president.

Thomas Paine (1737-1809) wrote directly to the average American colonist. Paine "wanted to persuade his readers of their human rights and democratic equality, and he wanted them to abandon the discredited ideas of hereditary rule, rank, and privilege" (Fruchtman, 2003, p.vii). His books, *Common Sense* and *Rights of Man* inspired not only the American Revolution but the French Revolution as well.

Thomas Jefferson (1743-1826) was a diplomat, inventor, architect, archaeologist, paleontologist, and founder of the University of Virginia, in addition to drafting the Declaration of Independence, serving as the second vice president under John Adams, and serving as the third president of the United States. Jefferson knew many of the Enlightenment thinkers personally. He was a strong believer in limited government.

George Washington (1732-1799) was the father figure that Americans needed. He was six feet, four inches tall and was respected in any room he entered. He didn't say much, but when he spoke everybody listened.

The American Revolution

The American Founding Fathers were reluctant rebels. They realized the English government was the most liberal on earth. They believed what their fellow Englishman, John Locke, said a few decades earlier—man has inalienable rights to life, liberty, and property. Keep in mind, the Founding Fathers still thought of themselves as English subjects, so they believed Locke was speaking to them.

The Declaration of Independence, penned by Jefferson, spoke of the inalienable rights to life, liberty, and the pursuit of happiness. The Americans believed that even without property you have an inalienable right to pursue happiness.

The Declaration of Independence meant, of course, war with England. The Founding Fathers risked everything in hopes of establishing a country based upon individual rights. The slavery debate between the Founding Fathers was shelved because losing the war would mean each "Founding Father" (or "rebel," if you were British) would be executed as a traitor (abolitionists and slave owners alike).

General George Washington was a wise military commander. He knew he could not defeat the British in a toe-to-toe fight. His strategy was to prolong the war long enough for Benjamin Franklin to convince the French to come to the aid of the Americans against the British.

Fortunately, for independence-seeking Americans, the French joined General Washington at Yorktown and the British finally surrendered. Years of Washington's hit-and-run tactics in the north, and American General Nathaniel Greene's seemingly endless "wild goose chases" (with only a small band of American rebels) throughout the south, convinced the exhausted and nearly bankrupt British to grant independence to the Americans.

The Constitution and Bill of Rights

The form of government chosen by the American Founding Fathers built upon separation of powers was not dramatically different from England's. The Constitution employed many of the ideas of John Locke and the Enlightenment thinkers.

The Bill of Rights made it clear that America would have a limited government. In America, the individual would be sovereign. The state would serve the individual, not the other way around.

Many Americans in the early twenty-first century, including me, regret that many of these rights have been lost. As Jefferson predicted, "Government will grow at the expense of individual liberties."

The French Revolution

While the American Revolution led to the loss of life for many soldiers, it did not turn into the horrific bloodbath of the French Revolution. The American Revolution was not a bloodless revolution like the "Glorious Revolution" of 1688 in England, but fortunately the Americans and English shared a similar real-world philosophy that limited the bloodshed. After the American Revolution, the Americans and English quickly re-established trade and diplomatic relations.

Remember that I said earlier that the Continentals, including the French, followed the Platonic "rationalist" tradition. This dramatically affected the outcome of the French Revolution, even after the American Revolution had succeeded. The Platonic-rationalist tradition is obvious in the earlier work of René Descartes (the father of modern French philosophy).

With the Platonic utopian mindset, the French found it impossible to establish the principles of liberty in the real world. The same mindless use of the guillotine to kill the aristocrats led to the use of the guillotine to kill the revolutionaries themselves. The ignorant leadership of the rabble collapsed into chaos.

The failure to establish a utopian brotherhood created a vacuum that was filled by Napoleon. Napoleon then rampaged throughout Europe. The devastation across Europe ended in the restoration of King Louis XVI to the throne in France. Millions of people died. The Continental Europeans, to this day, still do not understand the principles of individual rights and limited government.

The Counter-Enlightenment

During any great movement there is always a counter-movement. Just as the Reformation had its Counter-Reformation, the Enlightenment had its Counter-Enlightenment. Whereas the Enlightenment was based on reason, the Counter-Enlightenment was based upon emotion and utopian ideas.

The very influential leader of the Counter-Enlightenment in France was Jean Jacques Rousseau (1712-1778). Rousseau despised reason and spoke of "the noble savage" and anarchy. Rousseau believed discipline, rational thinking, and self-control were the "negative" results of an orderly society; he preached a return to a "state of nature." He thought we should live as animals or savages.

After reading one of Rousseau's manuscripts, Voltaire sent Rousseau the following response: "I have received, monsieur, your new book against the human race, and thank you for it. Never has so much intelligence been deployed in an effort to make us beasts. One wants to walk on all fours after reading your book" (Spencer & Krauze, 2006, p. 83).

Rousseau's anti-reason philosophy appealed to many in France. The French people paid a terrible price for their devotion to Rousseau. The French Revolution was a disaster, even after the American Revolution succeeded.

Unfortunately, utopian and Platonic fantasies did not end with Rousseau and the failure of the French Revolution. The German philosophers were about to take Plato's vision of an all-powerful State to unimaginable extremes.

Kant and the German Statists

I am going to be especially harsh with the German philosophers. I am of German descent myself. I was raised in a German-American family, and I felt a certain allegiance to German tradition in my youth. But after seriously studying philosophy for many years, I now realize how misguided and dangerous German philosophy is.

As I said earlier, the rationalists are not rational in the sense that the word "rational" is used in this book. They are irrational. The rationalist philosophers are better understood as "anti-empirical." I'll explain that momentarily.

Immanuel Kant

Will Durant (1953, p.192) characterizes Kant's influence with the following comments:

> "Never has a system of thought so dominated an epoch as the philosophy of Immanuel Kant dominated the thought of the nineteenth century."

> "To adapt Hegel's phrase about Spinoza: to be a philosopher, one must first have been a Kantian."

> "Schopenhauer calls *The Critique [of Pure Reason]* the most important work in German literature."

> "Nietzsche takes Kant for granted."

If you understand the anti-individual beliefs of Kant, those quotes are truly terrifying.

Immanuel Kant (1724-1804) spent his entire life in the city of Königsberg in Prussia. Kant, the "rationalist," epitomized the anti-empirical (anti-experience) philosopher. He saw no need to travel; he believed truth could be worked out in his head.

Prussia was a Germanic state known more for its military than its philosophy. Prussia was Lutheran; Kant was a Pietist, a very strict Protestant sect. Kant's work on ethics is an attempt to justify his Pietistic beliefs.

Kantian Ethics

Kant's ethical theory is deontological ("deon" is the Greek word for duty). According to Kant, duty is the only way you can justify your existence in this world. "An action is moral, according to Kant, only if one has no desire to perform it, but performs it out of a sense of duty and derives no benefit from it of any sort, neither material nor spiritual; a benefit destroys the moral value of an action" (Rand, 1961, p.32). So much for doing the right thing simply because you want to.

"It is the lot of the moral man to burn with desire and then, on principle—the principle of duty—to thwart it. The hallmark of the moral man is to suffer" (Peikoff, 1982, p.75). Kant does not allow you to simply live a law-abiding life in which you pursue your own goals; you must be miserable.

Kant's sacrificing ethical theory has been adopted by every tyrannical State. Hitler and Stalin preached Kantian ethics in every speech. Who benefits from all of this self-sacrificing? Answer: Whoever controls the State. The power of the State grows as individuals sacrifice their rights and resources. Utopian-State visions cannot be fulfilled without self-sacrifice on a grand scale.

Hegel and Marx

Georg W.F. Hegel (1770-1831), following in the Kantian philosophical tradition, was a major influence on Karl Marx. Even Hegel's fans admit to Hegel's obscurities and contradictions. Subsequent philosophers who disagreed on almost everything claim to be Hegelian.

Hegel's other-worldliness and idealism, like Kant's, make his works almost impossible to read. Also like Kant, as a "rationalist" (anti-empiricist), he feels no need to give real-world examples to support his theory. Hegel and Kant both believe truth does not have to correspond to physical reality, since they both believe physical reality is unknowable anyway.

Like Plato, Hegel grew up in a time of political instability. He watched the failure of the French Revolution in neighboring France. He watched the rise of Napoleon and the Napoleonic Wars; and then he saw the fall of Napoleon and the restoration of the Bourbon kings. Like Plato, he was a mystical utopian who believed in a powerful State.

Karl Marx (1818-1883) took Hegel's idea of history moving toward something grand and made it part of his vision of a utopian communist State. The Stalinist Communists in Russia and the Maoist Communists in China tried to implement Marx's political vision. Hitler's National Socialists tried to implement Marx's vision in Germany, but they substituted race for class.

I'll have more to say about Marx in the next chapter.

American Pragmatism

American philosophy degenerated from that of the Founding Fathers and the individuality of the 1800s into what is now known as Pragmatism. Pragmatism states that there is no such thing as objective truth, or even objective reality.

The rejection of objective reality is rooted in Kantian metaphysics (What is the nature of reality?). Kant said you cannot know the ding-an-sich (the thing-in-itself). For example, you cannot "know" the chair you are sitting in as it really is. You can only know your perceptions of the chair. In some sense, of course, this is true. But Kant takes this (and everything else) to nonsensical extremes. You don't know yourself; you only know your perceptions of yourself. You have no way of knowing if the thing-in-itself (or you) actually exists. You can see how all rational thinking can break down in post-Kantian philosophy.

Pragmatists believe truth is that which works; there are no enduring principles. As a principle-less philosophy, Pragmatism inevitably leads to quick fixes, short-term "solutions" with long-term disasters, and mob rule.

Pragmatism, Kantian ethics, and unlimited democracy can lead to the loss of all individual rights. If the individual must sacrifice all of his/her desires and values to the collective, the whims of the collective will rule with absolute authority. With no appeals to principles, such as inalienable individual rights, the individual becomes the slave of the collective.

American Pragmatism labels any individual with convictions or principles as dogmatic. In the early twenty-first century in the U.S., "truth" is determined by majority vote (mob rule). The American Pragmatists adopted the philosophy of collectivism from the German and Platonic traditions.

Peikoff wrote, "In the whirling Heraclitean flux which is the pragmatist's universe, there are no absolutes. There are no facts, no fixed laws of logic, no certainty, no objectivity" (1982, p.126).

Peikoff summarizes the philosophy of John Dewey, one of America's leading Pragmatists, with the following quote from Dewey: "There is no certainty—the very quest for it is a fundamental aberration, a perversion" (Peikoff, 1982, p.126).

In the early twenty-first century, individualists are outcasts in America; individuals are expected to absorb prevailing popular beliefs without question. This "pragmatic" approach applies in education, politics, and in society in general. The mob rules.

Conclusion

The purpose of this chapter on the history of political philosophy is to reveal the two opposing schools of political philosophy: statism and individualism. These two schools of thought are mutually exclusive. They cannot co-exist. One will win; one will lose. Currently, in America, statism is winning.

Statism can be traced to its roots in Plato's philosophy. Immanuel Kant added an ethical argument to destroy the individual. The German Statists, led by Hegel and Marx, developed the vision that was adopted by Hitler's National Socialists and Stalin's Communists. Socialism, in the forms of fascism and communism, failed catastrophically. But socialism continues to live in the form of American Pragmatism. Socialism, by its nature, will lead to an all-powerful statist government where individuals have no rights.

Individualism was introduced, in the form of property rights and the freedom to think rationally, in Aristotle's philosophy. John Locke, the Scottish Enlightenment thinkers, and the French Enlightenment thinkers advocated individual rights in Europe from 1690 to 1790. The American Founding Fathers took up the cause of individual liberty and implemented the philosophy of rational individualism on a large scale.

Rational individualism has been under attack by the collectivists, statists, and socialists operating in America during the 20th and 21st centuries. Fortunately, defenders have risen to the challenge. Libertarians and free-market capitalist economists have taken a stand for individualism.

References

Durant, Will (1953). *The Story of Philosophy*. New York: Simon and Schuster.

Fruchtman, Jack (2003). "Foreword," *Common Sense, Rights of Man, and Other Essential Writings of Thomas Paine*. New York: Signet Classics.

Peikoff, Leonard (1982). *Ominous Parallels*. New York: Plume.

Rand, Ayn (1961). *For the New Intellectual*. New York: Signet.

Spencer, Lloyd & Krauze, Andrzej (2006). *Introducing the Enlightenment*. Cambridge, UK: Icon Books.

CHAPTER 6

A Brief History of Economics

As WE HAVE SEEN throughout this book, there are two mutually exclusive ideologies that can be traced throughout human history: the ideology of individualism/ libertarianism/capitalism and the ideology of collectivism/ statism/socialism.

In philosophy, the terms used in the debate are individualism versus collectivism. In politics, the terms used are libertarianism versus statism.

In economics, the debate is between the capitalists and the socialists. Whereas the debate in philosophy can be traced back thousands of years to Plato and Aristotle, the debate in economics can be traced back only a few hundred years to Adam Smith in the late 1700s.

Prior to Adam Smith, it was assumed that the individual was part of a collective (tribe, city-state, or country); he/she sacrificed all individual rights to the State (chief, king, or government) in exchange for protection. Before Adam Smith there wasn't even a debate.

Adam Smith

Adam Smith (1723-1790), the father of modern economics, was a Professor of Moral Philosophy (what we now call "Ethics") at the University of Glasgow in Scotland. His second book, *The Wealth of Nations* (published in 1776), has been the starting point for every economic argument (either for or against) ever since.

All capitalists, including me, see Smith as an intellectual father. Smith believed his economic model would result in "universal opulence which extends itself to the lowest ranks of the people" (Smith, 1965/1776, p.11). His argument about greater wealth for everybody by increasing the size of "the pie" (creating wealth) is rejected by the socialists, but embraced by capitalists. Collectivists, statists, and socialists prefer re-distributing the current "pie" (available resources) rather than increasing the size of the pie (creating new wealth).

More than one hundred years after Smith, Andrew Carnegie (the American industrialist) said, "Capitalism is about turning luxuries into necessities." We know the greatest fortunes have been made by people who took new innovations and figured out how to make them available to the common person. Yes, Smith's capitalism benefits everybody.

Mercantilism

Adam Smith's great book was written in reaction to the European economic policies of his time. Smith lived when the economic system dominating Europe was mercantilism. "The mercantilists believed that the world's economy was stagnant and its wealth fixed, so that one nation grew only at the expense of another" (Skousen, 2001, p.17). Not surprisingly, European countries were constantly at war.

In the mercantilist mind, exports must be encouraged while imports must be discouraged. They sought a "positive" balance of trade. This ridiculous policy is still central to socialist economic policy today. Common sense tells us to produce and sell what we are good at, and to purchase everything else. If the French produce better wine at a lower price than we can, we should buy our wine from the French.

Free Trade

Smith was against trade barriers. He correctly believed trade barriers help only inefficient domestic producers.

Free trade benefits everybody. Smith saw economic freedom as a human right.

What Smith called "natural liberty" included:

- the right to buy goods from any source (domestic or foreign)

- the right to be employed in any occupation a person wants

- the right to move from one town to another

- the right to charge whatever price a buyer is willing to pay

- the right to save and invest accumulated wealth

These are rights which must be exercised without governmental restraint.

The Nobel Prize-winning economist George Stigler (1911-1991) called Smith's model of competitive free enterprise, individuals pursuing their self-interests under conditions of competition, the "crown jewel" of *The Wealth of Nations* (Stigler, 1976). This principle is the cornerstone of free market economics to this day.

The "Invisible Hand"

Adam Smith envisioned free individuals pursuing their self-interests and appealing to the self-interests of others in a free market. His concept of enlightened self-interest is referred to as the "invisible hand."

The following two quotes demonstrate how Smith believed rational self-interest led to a better society for everybody: "It is not from the benevolence of the butcher, the brewer, or the baker, that we expect our dinner, but from their regard to their own interest. We address ourselves, not to their humanity, but to their self-love." Smith then added, "[L]ed by an invisible hand to promote an end which was no part of his intention... by pursuing his own interest he frequently promotes that of the society" (Smith, 1965/1776, pp.42 & 423).

Smith was a libertarian, not an anarchist. He believed a strong but limited government was a necessity. The critical roles of government were to provide a legal system to protect individual rights and property rights, and to enforce contracts. These are the only legitimate roles of government in the economy. The government is not the "invisible hand." The invisible hand is the enlightened self-interests of all individuals in the marketplace.

Smith also believed a gold and/or silver standard was an important control against government intervention into the economy. He feared that governments would inflate their economies by printing enormous amounts of currency. Citizens of every country ever since have suffered by not heeding Smith's warning.

To Save or Not To Save

Adam Smith advocated hard work and thrift. He believed the savings of individuals became the essential capital needed for economic growth. In the 20th century, John Maynard Keynes attempted to overthrow Smith's Classical Economics model with his anti-savings model. As I write these words in the early 21st century, the United States is on the verge of bankruptcy. We should have listened to the professor from Scotland!

Say and Bastiat

In the previous chapter, we looked at the major contributions of the French Enlightenment thinkers to the American Founding Fathers and to the cause of individual liberty. In this chapter, we return to France to hear from French economic thinkers, who not only agreed with Smith's Classical Economics model, but who actually improved it.

During the twelve years it took Adam Smith to write *The Wealth of Nations,* he spent time in France discussing his ideas with French intellectuals such as Voltaire, Quesnay, and Turgot. No doubt their ideas influenced Smith's thinking; they certainly shared Smith's worldview.

The next generation of French thinkers, including Say and Bastiat, lived after the successful American Revolution and the failed French Revolution. They lived in a different world than Smith's.

Jean-Baptiste Say and Frédéric Bastiat rejected Smith's labor theory of value. As well they should; Smith was wrong. This one misstep by Smith opened the door for endless Marxist ranting and raving about the exploitation of workers.

J.B. Say

Jean-Baptiste Say (1767-1832) "was a major supporter of Adam Smith's self-directed economic system of competition, natural liberty, and limited government. He was an uncompromising defender of laissez-faire capitalism" (Skousen, 2001, p.49). Say's unyielding stand put him at odds with Napoleon. Napoleon, a caricature of a statist, banned Say's textbook.

"In 1815, after the fall of Napoleon, J-B Say became France's first professor of industrial economics" (Skousen, 2001, p.49). Say was now allowed to speak, and many listened.

Say believed no amount of labor or production determines value. He was a forerunner of the utility theory of value. Say believed value was determined by the user, not the producer.

Say declared, "a product is no sooner created, than it affords a market for other products to the full extent of its value" (Say, 1971/1803, p.134). A producer who produces and sells a product is also a buyer (consumer) with spendable income. To buy, you must first sell! Thus, Say's "Law of Markets" states production (supply) precedes consumption (demand). According to Say, buyers need to produce before they become consumers. Production spending is always a leading indicator; production spending precedes consumer spending. During an economic downtown, the need is for more producers (more capital investment in production).

In 1821, Thomas Jefferson had Say's textbook translated into English. "Say's English edition was the most popular textbook in the United States until it was superseded by John Stuart Mill's textbook following the Civil War" (Skousen, 2001, p.49).

Bastiat

Frédéric Bastiat (1801-1850) was a vocal opponent of socialism and statism. "Using entertaining fables, the French essayist attacked statism of all kinds—socialism, communism, utopianism, and mercantilism" (Skousen, 2001, p.59). Bastiat's famous *Broken Window* fable was adopted by Henry Hazlitt in his best-selling book, *Economics in One Lesson* (1979/1946).

Bastiat, like Adam Smith, grew up in a port city and saw the problems of government intervention. In his work, Bastiat demonstrates how government control of private industry and individuals was inefficient, counterproductive, and morally wrong.

Like today's libertarians, Bastiat believed the proper role of government is defending the rights to life, liberty, and property of its individual citizens. (I highly recommend that you read *Selected Essays on Political Economy* [1995], a collection of Bastiat's work, published by the Foundation for Economic Education [FEE]. In fact, I would recommend anything published by FEE.)

Bastiat was not an anarchist, but a libertarian. He believed government was a necessity, but that it must be limited. He warned about the seductive lure of socialism, a slow but sure path to destruction. His concept of creeping socialism is reflected in F.A. Hayek's book, *The Road to Serfdom* (2007/1944).

Bastiat also spoke out against slavery and all forms of government sanctioned "legal plunder" (tariffs, subsidies, guaranteed jobs, minimum wages, and forced charity or what I've called "legalized extortion").

David Ricardo

After a solid foundation was built for modern free markets by Smith, Say, and Bastiat in the late 18th and early 19th centuries, you would think we'd live in a prosperous, peaceful world of free trade and individual freedom in the 21st century. Not so.

As I've said throughout this book, the advocates of the anti-individual, anti-freedom philosophy of socialism and statism have sought control throughout history. These advocates want to control society and the State. No amount of evidence in this book, or from anywhere else, will convince them to abandon their quest for power.

David Ricardo (1772-1823) was four years old when *The Wealth of Nations* was published. In many ways, Ricardo was a disciple of Adam Smith. Unfortunately, many of Ricardo's worst ideas were adopted by Karl Marx and the socialists. Marx considered Ricardo to be his intellectual mentor.

Ricardo was a brilliant man, but his writing is extremely abstract with complicated mathematical formulas. Ricardo rarely used examples to relate his theory to the real world. Like the German Statists philosophers discussed in the last chapter, Ricardo was a believer in the coherence theory of truth; he believed his abstract theory could be true without corresponding to the real world. This seems strange when you consider how Ricardo became fabulously wealthy. David Ricardo had a practical side. He made his fortune in the stock and bond markets as a stockjobber. Many historians call him a stockbroker, but that's not correct. A stockjobber trades for his own accounts, not for customer accounts. To be exact, Ricardo's fortune was primarily made in government bonds and loans, often at great risk. Ricardo bet big on Wellington's defeating Napoleon. Both Ricardo and Wellington won big.

By the age of 40, an extremely wealthy Ricardo lost his interest in the stock and bond markets. He devoted the last decade of his life to abstract economics.

Got It Right

Ricardo rarely used examples, but one in particular was great. In one famous case he proves the value of free trade and the importance of labor specialization (Ricardo, 1951/1817). The case shows how two countries can increase total wealth by specializing in what they do best. While the example itself is beyond the scope of this book, it is still used in classrooms today.

Ricardo was right about advocating free trade, division of labor, and what caused inflation. Ricardo correctly stated that inflation was caused by the government (or its central bank) issuing too much currency. Many libertarians, including me, support this quantity theory of money.

Got It Wrong

When Ricardo got it wrong, he was very wrong. Unfortunately, his mistakes were very influential. Ricardo's devout followers included Karl Marx, Marxist economists, and a host of socialism's most vocal advocates.

Ricardo promoted the labor theory of value (as opposed to the utility theory of value). His "iron law of wages" later became the foundation for the Marxian myth of the exploited worker. Because he believed there was an inverse relationship between profits and wages, Ricardo provided future Marxists with ammunition for class warfare. Ricardo was especially critical of landlords.

Where Smith's economic model promoted harmony, Ricardo's model promoted disharmony and conflict. Bitter, anti-establishment types, like Marx, found fuel for their rage in the work of Ricardo.

I also want to accuse Ricardo of derailing the study of economics. The study of economics should be fascinating and practical. Unfortunately, the study of economics at many universities has become convoluted and irrelevant because of the overuse of econometrics. Econometrics is a result of the

Ricardian tradition of abstract model-building, often with no empirical evidence to support conclusions.

John Stuart Mill

To say that John Stuart Mill (1806-1873) and his father, James Mill (1773-1836) were disciples of Ricardo seems like an understatement. Ricardo bequeathed a large sum of money to James Mill. Ricardo had a big influence on James and John Stuart.

Both of the Mills were also influenced by the bizarre philosopher Jeremy Bentham (1748-1832). Bentham, a close friend of James, was one of the founders of the philosophy of Utilitarianism. Utilitarians advocate a hedonistic calculus to determine what is right. Put simply, the right decision is whatever benefits the majority. Obviously, this is fine if you are in the majority, but unfortunate (even deadly) if you are in the minority.

Bentham inherited wealth and became a self-proclaimed philosopher. Bentham encouraged the building of panopticons for his ideal society. A panopticon was designed so that an overseer could watch every movement throughout a facility. Bentham advocated his panopticons for prisons, workhouses, factories, insane asylums, and schools (Rothbard, 1995, pp. 62-64). Bentham envisioned three-fifths of the British people being controlled by his panopticons.

Bentham is perhaps the weirdest man who ever lived. Bentham agreed to make a large donation to University College in London if they agreed to put his stuffed corpse in a movable display case at the university. The movable display case was to be wheeled into the annual meetings. You can still visit Bentham's dead body at University College in London, but I hope you have no desire to do so.

John Stuart Mill's Personal Life

If you combine the influence of Ricardo, Bentham, and a heartless taskmaster of a father, you'd expect to find a deeply disturbed young man. You'd be right.

John Stuart had few friends, never participated in games, and had a nervous breakdown at 20. He often contemplated suicide.

At the age of 24 (1830) he began a relationship with a married woman named Harriet Taylor. Harriet's husband approved of and financed the relationship. He bought a country cottage for John and Harriet and paid for their trips abroad. The relationship remained purely platonic until Harriet's husband died in 1851. This story seems unbelievable until you know that John's friends described him as a "chilly, bloodless man, over-intellectual, under-sexed, uxorious, priggish and humourless" (Stafford, 1998, p.23).

Got It Right

Many libertarians speak of John Stuart Mill as if he were one of us. He's not. Mill spoke out against slavery in America and for women's suffrage. He should be applauded for those stands. Like Ricardo, Mill supported Adam Smith's system of natural liberty and Say's law of markets (Skousen, 2001, p.123).

Got It Wrong

But Mill was a Ricardian. He believed profits and wages were inversely correlated (which supported Marxian economics). In his book, *Principles of Political Economy* (1848), Mill stated that society should redistribute wealth without regard for who produced it. Mill was clearly a socialist who laid the foundation for the destructive work of future socialists and statists.

Friedrich Hayek (whom we will visit later) said, "I am person-ally convinced that the reason which led the intellectuals to socialism was John Stuart Mill" (Boaz, 1997, p.50).

Karl Marx

Perhaps the two most hateful men who ever lived were Karl Marx (1818-1883) and his collaborator/financial supporter Friedrich Engels (1820-1895).

"In the name of human progress, Marx has probably caused more death, misery, degradation, and despair than any man who ever lived" (Downs, 1983, p.299). When you consider all of the failed Marxist regimes in Russia, China, Cambodia, eastern Europe, and throughout the rest of world, that's a fair statement.

The Personal Marx

While he accused capitalism of exploitation, he "exploited everyone around him—his wife, his children, his mistress and his friends" (Payne, 1968, p.12). He supposedly cared about the working man, but he never held a steady job or even visited a factory.

During his college years he was known for drunkenness, carousing, accumulating debts, participating in revolution-ary groups, gun fighting (he was wounded in a duel), being ruthlessly opinionated, having a violent temper, and for being arrested on several occasions. His obviously embarrassed father had to move Karl from the University of Bonn to the University of Berlin. Karl eventually earned his doctorate in Greek phi-losophy from the University of Jena. All of this was financed by his father. Karl never showed any gratitude.

Marx was even worse in marriage. At the age of 25 he married Jenny Westphalen. Jenny's patience with Karl is beyond imagination. Even though Karl had a doctorate he refused to seek a teaching position or any other form of employment. In a lifetime of arrests and exiles, Marx moved his wife and six children around Europe. In one example, Marx was arrested by the Belgian police for spending his father's inheritance to arm Belgian workers with rifles. "Three of Marx's young children died of malnutrition and illness" (Skousen, 2001, p.143).

Then there was the affair with his wife's unpaid servant, Helene Demuth. Helene gave birth to a son. Even though the boy looked like Karl, Marx convinced his wealthy friend, Friedrich Engels, to pretend to be the boy's father. When one of Marx's daughters learned the truth, she committed suicide. A second daughter also committed suicide, but Marx's supporters say there's no proof that was Marx's fault.

Saul Padover, a Marx biographer, described the Marx family living in squalor—thick dust, coal smoke, and tobacco fumes. They were constantly broke. And Karl believed "washing, grooming, and changing underwear" unnecessary (Padover, 1978, pp.291-93). How did Jenny, Karl's wife, endure this life-style? I can't imagine.

Anti-Semitic

Marx has been called a self-hating Jew. Both of his parents were Jewish. In 1843, Marx wrote a defamation of the Jews entitled *On the Jewish Question*. Marx's slander of the Jews was lifelong. "His letters are replete with anti-Semitic remarks, caricatures, and crude epithets: 'Levy's Jewish nose,' 'usurers,' 'Jew boy,' 'nigger-Jew,' etc." (Padover, 1978, p.171).

Religion

Marx was a vicious opponent of religion. But, many of his beliefs are simply biblical passages twisted to his purposes. Skousen states, "Marxism has become a quasi-religion, with its slogans, symbols, red banners, hymns, party fellowship, apostles, martyrs, bible and definitive truth" (2001, p.134). I disagree with Skousen only on the word "quasi." Marxism is a religion. Marxism must be accepted on faith.

Marxism has failed miserably everywhere it's been tried. Robert Wesson's book title says it all, *Why Marxism? The Continuing Success of a Failed Theory* (1976).

Plato, Kant, Hegel, Ricardo, and Mill

Marx was clearly influenced by Plato. Marx earned his doctorate in Greek philosophy. Marx envisioned implementing Plato's utopian Republic. To fulfill the vision, Marx saw the need for the anti-individual philosophy of Kant, the conflict model of progress of Hegel, the economic class struggle of Ricardo, and the utilitarianism of Mill.

Comrade Engels

Friedrich Engels idolized Karl Marx. They met in Paris and began a 40-year collaboration that didn't end until Marx's death in 1883. Engels was content to live in Marx's shadow, and continued to advocate Marx's doctrine until his own death in 1895.

Engels was the son of a wealthy German industrialist. He hated his domineering father. He described his father's business as "boring, dirty, and abominable" (Skousen, 2001, p.140). But he enjoyed the fruits of his father's business. He spent lavishly and was well-known for his womanizing.

Friedrich had the opportunity to run a textile factory himself. There is no evidence that he did anything to improve the conditions of his own "exploited" workers. Apparently, he did not think the idea of re-distributing wealth applied to "capitalists" like him, as long as they called themselves "communists."

Engels did re-distribute a lot of his wealth to Marx, but Marx could not be considered to be a worker because Marx never held a job. None of this money ever reached Marx's wife and children, but Karl always had money to buy a round of drinks.

At the age of 24, Engels wrote *The Condition of the Working Class in England in 1844*. It was Engels who converted Marx to revolutionary socialism, not the other way around. Engels also served as the coauthor of *The Communist Manifesto* with Marx in 1848.

If you are a socialist, or statist of any type, you owe a debt to Friedrich Engels.

The Bourgeois Marx

In 1856, Marx's mother-in-law (Jenny's mother) died and left a substantial estate to Jenny. Karl took advantage of the windfall and moved his family to a fashionable neighborhood in London. "Marx started living the life of a bourgeois gentleman, wearing a frock coat, top hat, and monocle. The Marxes gave parties and balls, and traveled to seaside resorts. Marx even played the stock market. He speculated in American shares and English joint-stock shares" (Skousen, 2001, p.143). I'm not even going to comment on this. Marx led a life of disgusting duplicity.

Das Capital

Marx's book *Das Capital* was published in German in 1867. Marx considered it to be the bible of the working class, but it's so theoretically abstract, dense, and divorced from the real-world, no worker (and few scholars) could possibly make any sense of it. Reviews were poor in Germany, so Engels and other supporters managed to get it translated into Russian (1872) and French (1875).

In 1890, the American edition, entitled simply *Capital*, became a best-seller in the U.S. It "sold out quickly because *Capital* was promoted as a book informing readers how to accumulate capital—a course on money making" (Padover, 1978, p.375). Knowing Marx's high ethical standards, aren't you surprised that Marx didn't stop such a marketing scam? (I'm joking, of course.)

Das Capital never became the bible of the working class, but it did become the bible of Vladimir Lenin. "Without Marx there would have been no Lenin, without Lenin no communist Russia" (Schwarzschild, 1947, p. vii).

Das Capital started a class war that continues to this day. Karl's purpose was to destroy the bourgeoisie and to promote his exploitation theory of capitalism.

Marx's Legacy

Marx built upon the class-struggle models of David Ricardo and John Stuart Mill to launch a never-ending war between the classes. The members of the successful class (the minority) will be forevermore attacked by the unsuccessful class (the majority) with weapons supplied by Marx.

Marx adopted Ricardo's labor theory of value to "prove" that profits were surplus value gained by exploiting workers. This justified Marx's declaration of war against capitalists. To this day, capitalists are on the defensive. You can see these Marxist attacks in the media every day.

Marx was anti-technology as well as anti-capitalist. He believed machinery and technology benefited the capitalist, but not the worker. Anti-technology and back-to-the-primitive movements still quote Marx. In reality, the only way workers can increase their wages is to increase their productivity. That requires technology.

Marxist anti-capitalist attitudes have devastated economies in South America, Asia, and Africa. Marxist beliefs in many countries have resulted in negative economic growth.

Marx's desire to abolish private property has led to the deterioration of buildings and countless properties worldwide. Public property belongs to nobody, so it is the responsibility of nobody. Public property is always abused.

Marx Today

The good news about Marx is that he has been proven wrong about everything. Countless obvious examples show the failure of Marxist theory. South Korea/North Korea and West Germany/East Germany are but two examples.

In the early 21st century, former Marxist countries are adopting capitalist policies and all of their citizens are living better. The middle class has not disappeared as Marx predicted; the middle class has expanded.

Mark Skousen writes about today's worker-capitalist phenomenon. Skousen states, "Fewer and fewer workers are simply employees or wage earners. They are often shareholders and part owners of the company they work for—through profit-sharing and pension plans, where they own shares" (2001, p.158).

But Marxism is not dead. The class war continues. Bitter, unsuccessful people still use Marx to attack successful people. Fortunately, we freedom-seeking capitalists have defenders too.

The Austrian School

The madness of Marx helped fuel many revolts throughout Europe in the 1800s, but the predictions of Marx were obviously wrong by the end of the century. London, where Marx lived, had become one of the wealthiest cities in human history because of the industrial revolution (not a Marxist revolution). All classes (capitalists, landlords, and workers) enjoyed better living standards. The common man for the first time in history experienced more than the basic necessities of life. Marx died in obscurity in 1883. The twelve-foot monument that marks his grave was erected by the Communist party in the 1950s.

After Ricardo, Mill, and Marx, serious rational thinking was necessary to re-establish the economic vision of Smith, Say, and Bastiat in the real world. This responsibility fell largely to the members of the Austrian school of economics.

Menger

In 1871, Carl Menger (1840-1921) published *Principles of Economics* (1976/1871). Menger's book launched the neo-classical school of economics, which combined Adam Smith's economic model with the marginal-utility theory of value.

The marginal-utility theory of value correctly states that value is determined by the individual user. Building upon Jean Baptiste Say's belief that no amount of labor or production can determine the value to the user, Menger added the concept of marginal value. Menger said the larger the quantity of any good available to an individual, the smaller the value of each additional unit. Thus, the utility value to the user is determined at "the margin." Menger believed there was a principle of diminishing marginal utility operating without regard to labor or production costs.

One of Adam Smith's mistakes in *The Wealth of Nations* was the distinction between value-in-use versus value–in-exchange. Marxists and socialists used Smith's erroneous dichotomy to argue that capitalists could engage in profitable exchange without regard to the users. The Marxist argument, of course, is nonsense because the two things cannot be separated in the real world.

The marginal-utility theory of value proved the Marxist labor theory of value to be wrong. Value is determined by the user. In the real world, profits and use cannot be separated. The producer must understand the value to the user; understanding labor and production costs alone is not enough.

The Austrian economists believed the marginal-utility theory of value could be applied to all factors of production—wages, rents, and profits. Demand established price. A warehouse full of widgets that nobody wants has a value of zero; the labor and production costs don't change the value to the user. An American political candidate once accused his opponent of "knowing the cost of everything, but the value of nothing." Cost does not equal value. Ricardo, Mill, and Marx were wrong.

Menger and the Austrians proved that value was subjective. There is no objective measure of value. As Skousen stated, "Ricardo's search for an invariable measure of value was like Ponce de Leon's search for the fountain of youth, all in vain" (2001, p.173). Ricardo and Marx were as lost as Ponce.

The Austrian concepts of marginal-utility, time preference, and opportunity cost should have completely destroyed the validity of all of Marxian economics. But there will always be power-seekers who resurrect dead ideas to serve their purposes.

Unfortunately, Menger and subsequent Austrians wasted enormous amounts of time in fruitless debate with the German

Historical School of economics over methodology. What came to be known as the Methodenstreit (methods battle) consumed countless hours that could have been better invested by the Austrians.

Böhm-Bawerk

Eugen Böhm-Bawerk (1851-1914) "was considered the best known economist on the continent at the turn of the century" (Samuelson, 1967, p.662). He was appointed to a professorship at the University of Innsbruck in 1880 and published *Capital and Interest* in 1884.

After his book *The Positive Theory of Capital* was translated into English in 1891, he was appointed to the Austrian Ministry of Finance. He was credited with cleaning up the finances of the government and returning the empire to the gold standard. (Too bad that he's not available to do the same thing for the United States.)

In 1896, Böhm-Bawerk wrote *Karl Marx and the Close of His System* (1984/1898). "His critiques were so devastating that Marxism has never really taken hold in the economics profession as it has in other disciplines (sociology, anthropology, history, and literary theory)" (Skousen, 2001, p.187).

According to Marx's theory of surplus value, workers deserved the full price of products produced. Marx believed capitalists, lenders, and landlords exploited the workers: capitalists didn't deserve profits, lenders didn't deserve interest, landlords didn't deserve rents.

Böhm-Bawerk proved Marx wrong on all three; capitalists, lenders, and landlords earned their profits, interest, and rents. Capitalists delay consumption of their earnings and invest those earnings in business ventures that benefit workers and consumers, often at considerable risk to the capitalists. The capitalist advances wages to his workers before the products are sold. "Therefore, argued Böhm-Bawerk, hired workers are rightly paid their *discounted* product or value" (Skousen, 2001, p.188).

Similarly, lenders are lending funds from somebody who has abstained from consuming current earnings. Böhm-Bawerk's "waiting argument" says interest income is compensation for individuals who lend their money (earnings) to others and then wait for a future date to consume their earnings. Likewise, landlords invest considerable funds and then wait for many years to recover their invested earnings.

Böhm-Bawerk believed workers must do more than just work hard to obtain a better standard of living; they must work smart. Workers must figure out how they can be more productive. Workers must also abstain from consuming all of their current earnings. Workers must be both "industrious and thrifty" (Böhm-Bawerk, 1959/1891, p.116). The Austrians, like Adam Smith, advocated savings and thrift.

Böhm-Bawerk left government service in 1904 and became a professor at the University of Vienna. Among his students were Ludwig von Mises and Friedrich Hayek. We will visit with his two famous students in a moment.

Many years ago, while traveling in Austria, I learned something interesting about the Austrian currency (and Austrian culture). Unlike the Americans, the Austrians did not limit the faces on their currency to government officials. I saw Austrian currency with the faces of psychologist Sigmund Freud and none other than Eugen Böhm-Bawerk!

Mises

The failure of economists (including John Maynard Keynes, who is discussed later) to predict the 1929 stock market crash and the Great Depression, left the western world looking for answers. Ludwig von Mises (1881-1973) had the answers.

"According to Mises, and his followers, the decision by central banks to inflate and reduce interest rates in the 1920s inevitably created an artificial boom" (Skousen, 2001, p.286). Mises, and his younger colleague Hayek, believed the international gold standard would inevitably turn the artificial inflationary boom into a bust. Needless to say, 1929-1933 proved them right.

Mises was the son of a prosperous Austrian railroad construction engineer. While a student at the University of Vienna, Mises read Menger's *Principles of Economics* and attended Böhm-Bawerk's seminars. After acquiring his Ph.D., Mises had hoped for a professorship at the University of Vienna. It was not to be for several reasons:

1. He was Jewish during a time of rising anti-Semitism.

2. He was a laissez-faire economist during rising socialism.

3. He was opposed to National Socialism.

After World War I, it looked as if Bolshevik-Communist revolutions were going to break out in every major European city. Otto Bauer took control of "Red Vienna" and it appeared that all of Austria would go communist. Mises convinced Bauer that a Marxist Austria would lose the critical help of the Americans and British. Mises later claimed he single-handedly saved Austria from communism (Rothbard, 1988, p.31). I believed there is certainly some justification for this bold claim.

Mises had a simple solution for inflation. During the early 1920s, Austria and Germany attempted hyperinflation as a way to pay the crushing war reparations imposed by the Treaty of Versailles.

Both Mark Skousen and Friedrich Hayek tell a similar story about Mises. When it was obvious inflation was out of control, Austrian government officials and League of Nation representatives came to Mises and asked, "How do we stop inflation?" Mises handed them a piece of paper with an address written on it, and said, "Meet me there at midnight." Standing outside that address at midnight, Mises said, "Hear that noise? Turn it off!" They were standing outside the government printing office; currency was being printed non-stop around the clock. The government officials stopped the noise; inflation ended (Skousen, 2001, p.289; Hayek, 1994, p.70).

As early as 1924, Mises predicted the coming stock market crash and depression. He warned against easy credit but was ignored. As I write this book, I have been warning against easy credit and artificially low interest rates (created by the Federal Reserve); like Mises, I'm being ignored.

As early as 1927, Mises predicted the end of freedom in Central Europe. Many listened to his advice and moved to England or the United States. In 1934, Mises accepted a position at the Graduate Institute of International Studies in Geneva, Switzerland. After six years in Switzerland, Mises and his family moved to the U.S.

In 1938, the Nazis invaded Vienna and raided Mises' apartment. They packed up 38 cases of his library, writings, and personal documents. Fortunately, in 1990, Richard Ebeling (the President of the Foundation for Economic Education) found Mises' work among KGB files in Moscow (Skousen, 2001, p.297).

Mises' 900-page *Human Action* was published in 1949. Human Action (2007/1949) covers a very wide range of topics. Some of the chapters, such as the ones on methodology, may not be of interest to today's readers, but there is great wisdom to be found in this masterpiece.

Mises rejected econometrics (the use of mathematics to predict economic activity). He believed there was no such thing as quantitative economics. Mises said the social sciences (including the study of human behavior) must be separated from the physical sciences. While the behaviors of animals and things (such as chemical reactions) are predictable, the behaviors of human beings are unpredictable. I would add: Even if human behavior is predictable, we do not have the computing power and mathematical models to integrate an almost infinite number of variables. Hayek, Mises' younger colleague, called attempts to use physical science methodology (including mathematical models) to predict human behaviors as nothing more than scientism.

Personally, I think the most readable book by Mises is *The Anti-Capitalist Mentality* (2006/1956). I've recommended it to countless individuals who are looking for an introduction to libertarian thinking.

Hayek

Friedrich Hayek (1899-1992) was almost 18 years younger than Mises. Hayek was Mises' protégé and colleague for many years. Hayek was born in Vienna and earned two doctorates from the University of Vienna (in law and political science). Hayek read Mises' *Socialism* (1981/1922), an argument against socialism, when he was 23 years old. It had a lifelong effect.

Similar to Mises, Hayek said "an artificial increase in the money supply would send false signals to producers and consumers, creating an inflationary boom that would inevitably turn to a bust" (Skousen, 2001, p.295). Both Mises and Hayek knew the gold standard would restrain the growth in the money supply. Clearly, they were right. The artificial boom of the 1920s led to the Great Depression.

Mises and Hayek, of course, assumed a gold standard. In the 21st century, we no longer have a gold standard. We are forced by the government to use fiat money. But switching from the gold standard to fiat money does not eliminate the consequences that follow inflating the money supply. The current manipulation of the fiat money supply can delay the bust, but the inevitable bust that we will face in the 21st century will be far more catastrophic than the Great Depression.

Lionel Robbins (1898-1984) was so impressed by Hayek's explanation of the depression of 1929-1933 as the inevitable result of the "Roaring Twenties" unsustainable inflationary boom, he had Hayek appointed as a professor at the London School of Economics (LSE). That's quite shocking when you realize the LSE was founded by Fabian Socialists. Robbins led a revival of Austrian economics in England. He had Mises' *Theory of Money and Credit* (1981/1912) translated into English, and he published his own book entitled *The Great Depression* in 1934. Robbins correctly blamed the Great Depression on governmental monetary mismanagement.

While everybody was impressed by Hayek's prediction of the Great Depression, few people were willing to accept his solution for what to do about it. Hayek insisted on a non-intervention government policy. He believed interest rates, prices, and employment levels must be determined by the free market. In my own words, "We had the party, now we had to suffer the consequences."

In 1944, Hayek wrote his bestseller *The Road to Serfdom* (2007/1944). He warned about the seductive power of socialism. He showed how the road to serfdom was not found only in totalitarian countries like Germany, but was a possible path to destruction in all western democracies. *The Road to Serfdom* should be read by anybody who wants to remain free.

In 1974, Hayek won the Nobel Prize in economics for his 1930s work on monetary theory and the business cycle. It's nice to know that his rational thinking was finally recognized during his lifetime.

Unfortunately, the tough, do-nothing, non-intervention policy advocated by Hayek (and Mises) during the 1930s was not as appealing as the quick-fix policies of John Maynard Keynes. Keynes would forever change economic thinking by separating actions (of individuals, organizations, and governments) from consequences.

John Maynard Keynes

It is possible that John Maynard Keynes has done more to destroy rational thinking about economics and freedom than any other person, including Karl Marx. Whereas Marxism is rejected by most intelligent people as utopian, poorly argued, and disastrous in practice, Keynesianism requires serious, rational thinking to debunk. Keynesianism is so evil because it is so seductive. Many well-intentioned people want to believe Keynes is a viable quick-fix for economic pain.

John Maynard Keynes (1883-1946) was born the same year that Karl Marx died. Keynes carried on Marx's unrelenting attack on sound economics and rational thinking. The arrogant John Maynard was often asked how to pronounce his family name; his response, "Keynes, as in brains." Keynes was often wrong, but never in doubt.

As the 1930s depression continued, politicians sought economists with "answers." The goal became one of alleviating the current pain without regard for long-term consequences.

Americans who had visited Russia and Germany in the 1930s returned with stories of great prosperity and full employment. Perhaps the Soviet Socialists in Russia and the National Socialists in Germany were right, they said. These Americans believed Stalin and Hitler had the answers for America.

John Maynard Keynes took advantage of these turbulent times to attack capitalism in his 1936 book, *The General Theory of Employment, Interest and Money*. He said capitalism was inherently unstable and required government control. He spoke of the economy as an automobile requiring steering by a government bureaucrat. (It didn't concern Keynes that the driver was untrained or blind.)

Keynes rejected the nationalization of industry. Thus, Keynes' model more closely resembled that of Hitler's Nazi form of socialism than it did Stalin's Communist form of socialism. Like Hitler and Stalin, Keynes advocated massive government spending on public works projects. These policies, adopted by Franklin Roosevelt, ushered in American socialism.

It was Keynes who introduced the idea of huge government deficit spending that plagues Americans today. Keynes believed governments should run deficits during bad times and then repay the accumulated debts during the good times.

There's an obvious problem with Keynes' "temporary" deficit spending to be paid off during "good times." For political purposes, "good times" will never be declared because that would mean tightening-the-belt to pay off past debts; that doesn't get votes. Deficit spending will continue as long as a national emergency is in the public eye: war, war on poverty, war on drugs, war on terrorism, or war on war.

Many economists have called Keynes the savior of capitalism because he was against nationalizing industry, but even

Hitler agreed with that. Hitler was hardly a savior of free-market capitalism; neither was Keynes.

Henry Hazlitt correctly said that Keynes' *General Theory* "constitutes the most subtle and mischievous assault on orthodox capitalism and free enterprise that has appeared in the English language" (Hazlitt, 1977/1960, p.345). Keynes' advocacy of government intervention, the welfare state, central planning, and deficit spending is the most direct attack on capitalism since Marx.

Keynes was not trained in economics (he took only one course in economics at Cambridge), but because of his father's position he was appointed as Senior British Treasury official to the Versailles Peace Conference in 1919. After Versailles, he wrote The Economic Consequences of the Peace. It became a best-seller.

As I said earlier, Keynes failed to predict the stock market crash of 1929. He lost three-quarters of his family's net worth. He was one of the fortunate ones who could afford to hold on to his investments until prices rebounded.

Keynes was smart enough to do some "bottom fishing" after the stock market crashed and bought some companies and commodities with future potential. He was able to rebuild his wealth.

In all of Keynes' work, I agree with only one sentence, but this is one that every investor should heed: Keynes said, "My central principle of investment is to go contrary to general opinion, on the ground that, if everybody is agreed about its merits, the investment is inevitably too dear and therefore unat-tractive" (Moggridge, 1983, p.11).

Keynes was a regular guest on BBC radio where he attacked the gold standard and savers as hurting the economy. He took these opportunities to promote deficit spending, inflation, and government intervention.

Keynes began his attacks on Adam Smith's classical economics as early as 1926 in a speech entitled *The End of Laissez-Faire.* "Keynes adopted the Freudian thesis that money making was a neurosis" (Skousen, 2001, p.335). In 1931, Keynes was quite blunt about how he felt about money making: "a somewhat disgusting morbidity, one of the semi-criminal, semi-pathological propensities which one hands over with a shudder to specialists in mental disease" (Keynes, 1963/1931, p.369).

Keynes' General Theory is basically a book-length refutation of Say's Law of Markets (discussed earlier in this chapter). Clearly, Keynes never read Say's work, or because he was not trained in economics, Keynes did not understand Say's Law. Say's Law states the opposite of what Keynes claims; Say believed production (supply) creates its own demand (consumption).

Keynes' failure to understand Say's Law led him to conclude that consumer spending was more important than production spending. Thus, Keynes recommended printing more currency to put into the hands of consumers.

Keynes also ignored Say's emphasis on "productive" production. Say believed "unproductive" production led to layoffs, warehouses overflowing with inventory, and economic downturns. Keynes recommended massive government spending on anything—productive or wasteful. Keynes said pyramid-building, natural disasters, and wars create wealth (1973/1936, p.129). Keynes should have read Bastiat's *Broken Window* fable.

In *The General Theory*, Keynes advocated permanently low interest rates (held down by the government or its central bank), return to mercantilism in bad times (Adam Smith must have rolled over in his grave at that idea), and replacing the gold standard with fiat money (Keynes, 1973/1936).

Keynes' utopian vision included expanding credit until full employment was achieved and forcing interest rates to zero. Keynes "encouraged British housewives to go on a buying spree and government to go on a building binge" (Skousen, 2001, p.341). Keynes asked, "Why not pull down the whole of South London from Westminster to Greenwich, and make a good job of it . . . Would that employ men? Why of course it would!" (1963/1931, pp.151-154). You have to be drunk on Keynesianism if you think this is rational.

Paul Samuelson

Keynesian socialism did not die with Keynes in 1946. Paul Samuelson (born 1915) took up the Keynesian cause with the publication of *Economics* (the most successful textbook ever published). Samuelson's *Economics* was first published in 1948 (the 100th anniversary of *The Communist Manifesto*). Economics has gone through 18 editions and has been translated into more than 40 languages. Samuelson's book dominated economics classrooms for 50 years.

Samuelson said, "I don't care who writes a nation's laws—or crafts its advanced treaties—if I can write its economics textbooks" (1990, p.ix). Samuelson knew the power of introducing post-World War II students to Keynesianism.

Samuelson took his first class in economics at the University of Chicago. The class was taught by Aaron Director (Chicago's most libertarian economist). Samuelson must have missed a few classes.

Like Keynes, Samuelson was poor at predicting depressions. Whereas Keynes failed to predict the 1930s depression, Samuelson predicted a disastrous post-World War II depression, which never happened. As we all know, the U.S. economy boomed after WWII. Samuelson also predicted that the Soviet Union's economic performance would surpass that of the United States.

Samuelson won the Nobel Prize in economics in 1970. I assume he won based on his textbook defending Keynesianism. (Hayek did not win it until 1974. Friedman was passed over until 1976. Mises never won it at all.)

Samuelson seemed to enjoy mocking the savings-and-thrift advice of Adam Smith and Benjamin Franklin. He went so far as to call it a sin in his *Economics* textbook.

Samuelson advocated higher taxes on the wealthy. He believed the wealthy were too frugal, so a "progressive" tax structure would re-distribute wealth to the poor who spend everything they get. He also supported farm aid, unemployment compensation, and Social Security taxes.

Samuelson believed the national debt is not a burden. He argued, "We owe it to ourselves." That is like saying taxes are not a burden because "We pay it to ourselves." He also failed to recognize that much of the national debt is in the hands of foreign investors.

The failure of Keynes and Samuelson to see the value of savings is inexcusable. "Savings is simply another form of spending, not on current consumption, but on future consumption" (Skousen, 2001, p.368). Savings are critical for future production. Production is critical for consumption (Say's Law).

Keynesianism and Samuelson's advocacy of Keynesianism has been almost universally accepted by politicians. Politicians, in a quest for votes, seek quick fixes and easy answers. Socialism, in all its forms, seduces with quick fixes and easy answers.

The adoption of these policies has brought the United States to the brink of bankruptcy and hyperinflation as I write this book in the early 21st century. After decades of popularity, Keynes and Samuelson's brand of socialism finally faces reality.

Milton Friedman

Milton Friedman (1912-2006) won the Nobel Prize in economics in 1976 (on the 200th anniversary of the publication of *The Wealth of Nations*), but it was not without years of struggle. During the 1950s and 1960s, Friedman's free-market advocacy was seen as extreme.

There were other free-market advocates in the 1950s and 1960s, including Henry Hazlitt and Murray Rothbard. Henry Hazlitt's *Failure of the New Economics* (1973/1959) is an excellent page-by-page critique of Keynes' General Theory. But Hazlitt was ignored by the academic community because he was a journalist instead of an academic.

Murray Rothbard published several excellent works on economics, including *America's Great Depression* (1983/1963). In this 1963 book, Rothbard used quantitative research to support his explanation of the 1929-1933 crash and depression. He demonstrated how the Federal Reserve's easy-money policy created the artificial boom during the 1920s. But Rothbard was discredited by mainstream (Keynesian) economists because Rothbard described himself as an anarcho-capitalist. Rothbard's beliefs in anarchism damaged his reputation in the eyes of almost everyone.

Fortunately, the Keynesians and socialists could not ignore Milton Friedman. Friedman had impeccable credentials: Ph.D. from Columbia, University of Chicago professorship, the John Bates Clark Medal, and the Nobel Prize in economics.

While a student at the University of Chicago, Friedman met his lifelong friend and collaborator, George Stigler (who won the Nobel Prize in economics in 1982). He also met his future wife and collaborator, Rose Director (sister of the University of Chicago's libertarian economist Aaron Director).

Friedman taught at the University of Chicago from 1946 until 1977. In 1977, he joined the Hoover Institute at Stanford University, where he stayed until his death in 2006. During his 60-year career, Friedman made some remarkable contributions to free-market economics.

In 1963, Friedman published an amazing empirical study, *A Monetary History of the United States, 1867-1960*, along with his co-author Anna Schwartz. The book demonstrated the importance of monetary policy and proved that it was the government's mismanagement that caused the Great Depression, not a failure of the capitalist system. Keynesians and socialists were at a loss to deny Friedman's and Schwartz's conclusions.

Friedman did not limit his concepts to an academic audience. In *Capitalism and Freedom* (1982/1962), Friedman brought his free-market ideas to the general public. He also wrote a popular *Newsweek* magazine column from 1966 until 1984.

Perhaps Friedman's greatest contribution to the cause of free-market economics was his 1980 ten-part PBS television mini-series entitled *Free to Choose*. Millions of people watched the television series. It was Friedman's book of the same name, *Free to Choose* (1980), that convinced me of the power of free markets while I was serving as the Chief Financial Officer of a bank during the 1980s.

Skousen (2001) said Friedman "has done more than any other economist to reverse the Keynesian tide and reestablish the virtues of neoclassical economics" (p.397). While I do not agree with Friedman on everything (I disagree with him on his beliefs about gold), it is hard not to see Friedman as the David in a struggle against a Goliath. Friedman, barely five-feet tall, has to be the most effective debater for free-market capitalism ever.

Friedman's arguments destroyed the Keynesian arguments that we looked at earlier in this chapter. Did Friedman finally silence the advocates of socialism?

The Future of Economics

You would think the real-world validation of the economic theories of Adam Smith, Say and Bastiat, Mises and Hayek, and finally Friedman would have silenced the voices of socialism. The world has witnessed the fall of the Berlin Wall. We've seen the collapse of Soviet socialism, Maoist communism, and every other imaginable form of socialist debacle throughout the world. But the battle between capitalism and socialism is not over. I don't believe it will ever end.

As long as there are jealous, unsuccessful people, socialism will be a weapon used against successful people. Socialism (the "legal" extortion of the earnings of successful people by the government for the benefit of unsuccessful people) will always be favored by politicians and the uneducated masses. Since the majority of people are unsuccessful, politicians will always turn to socialism as a way to power.

Don't expect the battle between capitalists and socialists to ever end. If you are a freedom-seeking individualist, you will always have to fight for individual rights, limited government, and capitalism.

References

Boaz, David (1997). *Libertarianism: A Primer*. New York: Free Press.

Böhm-Bawerk, Eugen (1959/1891). *The Positive Theory of Capital*. South Holland, IL: Libertarian Press.

Böhm-Bawerk, Eugen (1984/1898). *Karl Marx and the Close of His System*. Philadelphia: Orion Editions.

Downs, Robert (1983). *Books That Changed the World* (Second Edition). New York: Penguin.

Friedman, Milton (1982/1962). *Capitalism and Freedom*. Chicago: University of Chicago Press.

Friedman, Milton & Friedman, Rose (1980). *Free to Choose*. New York: Harcourt.

Hayek, Frederich (1994). *Hayek on Hayek*. Chicago: University of Chicago Press.

Hayek, Frederich (2007/1944). *The Road to Serfdom, The Definitive Edition*. (Edited by Bruce Caldwell). Chicago: University of Chicago Press.

Hazlitt, Henry (1973/1959). *The Failure of the New Economics*. New York: Arlington House.

Hazlitt, Henry (1977/1960). *The Critics of Keynesian Economics* (2nd Edition). New York: Arlington House.

Hazlitt, Henry (1979/1946). *Economics in One Lesson*. New York: Three Rivers Press.

Keynes, John Maynard (1963/1931). *Essays in Persuasion*. New York: Norton.

Keynes, John Maynard (1973/1936). *The General Theory of Employment, Interest and Money*. (In the Collective Writings of John Maynard Keynes, Volume 7). London: Macmillian.

Menger, Carl (1976/1871). *Principles of Economics* (Translated by James Dingwall and Bert Hoselitz). New York: New York University Press.

Mises, Ludwig von (1981/1912). *The Theory of Money and Credit* (5th Edition). Indianapolis: IN: Liberty Fund.

Mises, Ludwig von (1981/1922). *Socialism* (6th Edition). Indianapolis: IN: Liberty Fund.

Mises, Ludwig von (2006/1956). *The Anti-Capitalist Mentality* (Edited by Bettina Bien Greaves). Indianapolis: IN: Liberty Fund.

Mises, Ludwig von (2007/1949). *Human Action* (Edited by Bettina Bien Greaves). Indianapolis: IN: Liberty Fund.

Moggridge, David (1983). "Keynes as an Investor." *The Collected Works of John Maynard Keynes* (Volume 12). London: Macmillan, 1-113.

Padover, Saul (1978). *Karl Marx: An Intimate Biography*. New York: McGraw-Hill.

Payne, Robert (1968). *Marx*. New York: Simon & Schuster.

Ricardo, David (1951/1817). *On the Principles of Political Economy and Taxation*. Edited by Piero Sraffa. Cambridge: Cambridge University Press.

Rothbard, Murray (1983/1963). *America's Great Depression* (4th Edition). New York: Richardson and Snyder.

Rothbard, Murray (1988). *Ludwig von Mises: Scholar, Creator, Hero*. Auburn, AL: Ludwig von Mises Institute.

Rothbard, Murray (1995). *Classical Economics: An Austrian Perspective on the History of Economic Thought*. New York: Edward Elgar.

Samuelson, Paul (1967). "Irving Fisher and the Theory of Capital." In *Ten Economic Studies in the Tradition of Irving Fisher* (Edited by William Fellner et al.). New York: John Wiley

Samuelson, Paul (1990). "Foreword." In *The Principles of Economics Course* (Edited by Phillips Saunders and William Walstad). New York: McGraw-Hill.

Say, Jean-Baptiste (1971/1803). *A Treatise on Political Economy*. (Translated from the 4th Edition). New York: Augustus M. Kelley.

Schwarzschild, Leopold (1947). *Karl Marx, the Red Prussian*. New York: Grosset and Dunlap.

Skousen, Mark (2001). *The Making of Modern Economics*. Armonk, NY: M.E. Sharpe.

Smith, Adam (1965/1776). *The Wealth of Nations* (The Modern Library Edition). New York: Random House.

Stafford, William (1998). *John Stuart Mill*. London: Macmillan.

Stigler, George (1976). The Successes and Failures of Professor Smith. *Journal of Political Economy*, 84:6 (December) pp.1199-1213.

Wesson, Robert (1976). *Why Marxism? The Continuing Success of a Failed Theory*. New York: Basic Books.

CHAPTER 7

The Moral Argument

THROUGHOUT THIS BOOK, I have described the two competing ideologies that have battled each other throughout history: the individualist/libertarian/capitalist and collectivist/statist/socialist. These are not simply matters of preference. A socialist society violates individual rights. Socialism is immoral.

Socialism is built upon collectivist arguments, such as Kant's belief that our only justification for living is to serve others. Collectivism demands the sacrifice of the individual. If an individual chooses to not self-sacrifice, the individual will be forced to submit in a socialist society.

Socialism always has, and always will, lead to an all-powerful State. Statism is necessary to enforce the "legalized" extortion that is part of socialism.

Successful, productive, self-reliant individuals will naturally choose libertarianism and capitalism. A libertarian government and a capitalist economy provide these individuals with freedom to earn a living in a competitive marketplace. They are limited only by their individual ability and initiative.

A libertarian government protects that individual's rights to life, liberty, property, and the pursuit of happiness. As long as the individual does not violate the rights of other individuals, he or she is free to do whatever he or she desires.

Unsuccessful, unproductive people will always want to share in the earnings of successful, productive people. Unsuccessful, unproductive people will naturally favor statism and socialism. These people want others (the collective) to take care of them. They are willing to sacrifice their freedom to the State and to accept dependent servitude. Like children, they do not accept self-responsibility.

As we've seen in the previous two chapters, *A Brief History of Political Philosophy* and *A Brief History of Economics*, the battle between these two ideologies has a long history. It is foolish to believe the battle will ever end. As long as we have both productive people and unproductive people, the two ideologies will be in conflict.

America's Ideal

The Enlightenment took place in Europe, but the Europeans, to this day, have never tried individual freedom. The Enlightenment writers, beginning with John Locke in 1690, spoke clearly about the value of individual freedom.

The most enlightened country in Europe in the 1700s was England. (The reason many Americans did not want to rebel against the English government.) During the 1700s, England offered more freedom to its citizens than any other European country. The Georgian Era (George I, George II, and George

III) endured for most of the century. While monarchs in the traditional sense, they at least had enough sense to know how wealth was created. Kings, governments, and bureaucrats do not create wealth; individuals create wealth. More individual freedom always leads to more wealth creation.

Voltaire, one of the leading French Enlightenment thinkers, described at length how much he admired the freedom of the English. England built its wealth on trade. At the same time, the government (non-productive by nature) grew dramatically in France, Prussia, Austria, and Russia.

In the 1770s many Americans did not want independence from England because they realized that the English trade policies led to great wealth in the British colonies. The American Founding Fathers, who had read the Enlightenment writers, believed that even more freedom and wealth were possible with less government.

The American Revolution led to less government. Less government (limited government) led to enormous prosperity. The Americans clearly saw the value of individual freedom and individual responsibility. The collectivist Europeans (the Continentals in particular) have never wanted to assume the individual responsibility that comes with individual freedom.

The Europeans still believe the State has a divine wisdom that they (as individuals) do not have. Europeans have been dependent on the State for centuries, while Americans have detested dependency on government.

So why do many Americans in the early twenty-first century want to adopt a philosophy of dependency and entitlement? Because great wealth invariably provokes envy and attacks from the unproductive.

Productive, motivated, hard-working people always create wealth (when they have the freedom to do so). Everybody benefits as a result of their wealth creation: new products, more products at lower prices, more jobs, new and better everything. Unfortunately, the unproductive don't have the intelligence or ethics to appreciate where the wealth comes from.

The "scarcity mentality" of the unproductive tells them that rich people must have taken wealth from poor people. And then, identifying themselves as the "oppressed" poor, they turn to government to get "their share." Equally unproductive politicians gladly join "the cause" to take what productive people have produced. The result of this process is obvious: unproductive government programs and salaries wasted on government bureaucrats.

The American economy will soon become as stagnant as the European economies if America allows the voting majority of unproductive Americans to exploit productive Americans. Americans should not seek equality of wealth, but equality of opportunity to create wealth, which requires a limited government that is focused on protecting individual rights. If America adopts European socialism, it will see its wealth and productivity decline. Americans must accept individual responsibility if they want individual freedom.

Who Is Responsible?

In the early twenty-first century, there are still many flag-waving Americans lining the streets of small towns and big cities on July 4th. They all say they are celebrating freedom, but they are blissfully throwing away their freedom with both hands.

Freedom requires self-responsibility. Individuals who are free are responsible for themselves. As soon as the individual turns the responsibility for his/her life over to the State, the individual ceases to be free. When the State takes the responsibility for your life, it also takes the authority. Some bureaucrat will now decide what is best for you.

The self-reliant, rational individualist is hard to find in America today. Today, most Americans do not want the responsibility for their retirement, health care, job security, or for the education of their children. They gladly turn these responsibilities over to the State; any failure can then be blamed on some incompetent bureaucrat.

Whatever happened to the image of Americans as rugged individualists? Americans are now seen as uneducated, piggish characters devoid of self-control. Giving up self-responsibility, or never assuming it as a young adult in the first place, has led millions of Americans to rally behind schoolyard bullies (politicians) to get schoolyard privileges (benefits of government programs). Please note that these privileges/benefits were not earned by these "children."

The wholesale exchange of individual freedom for government promises of security (and a share of unearned income) is accelerating. After millions have fought for freedom, are Americans now ready to give away their freedom for the promises of American socialist politicians?

Beware the Promises of Socialists

Eric Hoffer (2002/1951) gave us great insight into the anti-individual nature of mass movements. Hoffer believed the leaders of mass movements could easily convert what he called "the frustrated" (what I call "the unproductive") into ready-to-die fanatics for social causes in which the frustrated individual could abandon his "irremediably spoiled" self.

The unproductive (the unsuccessful) in society need a purpose to live for. Since the majority of individuals perceive their self as "irremediably spoiled," these people look for a purpose beyond the self. They want to be self-less because it's the self that they despise. Leaders of socialist movements use this knowledge to build their power base.

Hoffer said, "A man is likely to mind his own business when it is worth minding. When it is not, he takes his mind off his own meaningless affairs by minding other people's business" (2002/1951, p.14). A man (or woman) who is living an unproductive, "meaningless" life is ripe for picking by socialist leaders. What better cause could there be than tearing down the productive and successful people, if you can blame them for your own failure? Blaming somebody else for your failure is easier than taking responsibility for your failure. These unproductive failures are easily transformed into raging socialists.

Conclusion

Since the majority of people are unproductive, socialist ideas and politicians will always have great power in an unlimited democracy. The unproductive don't want freedom; they want security. "Unless a man has the talents to make something of himself, freedom is an irksome burden" (Hoffer, 2002/1951, p.31). The unproductive will gladly trade their freedom for socialist promises of "equality."

The morality of stealing from productive people will never be discussed by socialist politicians. These politicians are smart enough to realize that they must have productive people under their control. (Socialist politicians are immoral, not stupid.) Without productive people, unproductive people and their socialist politicians would starve to death.

In a socialist society, productive people become the "cattle" of the socialist rulers. Socialist politicians want the power to decide which cattle will be eaten. The cattle have no rights. In a socialist society, you will see "the sacrifice of productive genius to the demands of envious mediocrity" (Rand, 1990, p.256).

If you are a rational individualist, you must be vigilant. You must listen closely for political rhetoric that will rob you of your individual rights to life, liberty, property, and the pursuit of happiness.

The following table gives you an overview of the opposing concepts from both ideologies:

Individualism	Collectivism
Libertarianism	Statism
Capitalism	Socialism
Rational	Anti-rational
Individual Rights	"Group Rights"
Individual Freedom	Government Control
Private Property	Public Property
Productive People	Unproductive People
Seeking Freedom	Seeking Power
Empirical	Anti-Empirical
Correspondence Theory of Truth	Coherence Theory of Truth
Reality-Based	Wish-Based
Real World	Utopian

TABLE 7.1: *The Competing Ideologies*

This table can be used as a reference as you listen to the endless socialist rhetoric in the media. Don't be fooled; American socialism is alive and well.

What's a rational individualist to do? You must reject the easy (and immoral) solutions of the socialists. You must take complete responsibility for yourself.

Socialism is immoral. Capitalism is the only moral political-economic system.

References

Hoffer, Eric (2002/1951). *The True Believer: Thoughts on the Nature of Mass Movements.* New York: Perennial Classics.

Rand, Ayn (1990). *The Voice of Reason.* New York: Meridian.

Annotated Bibliography

I HAVE INCLUDED this annotated bibliography because I found these particular books to be the most insightful in my own study. The authors of these books believe strongly in individual rights, limited government, capitalism, and rational thinking.

Anderson, Benjamin (1980). *Economics and the Public Welfare*, (rev. ed.) Indianapolis, IN: Liberty Fund.

> The author, a business economist, explains how the government was the cause, not the cure, of the Great Depression.

Bastiat, Frédéric (1995/1848). *Selected Essays on Political Economy*. Irvington-on-Hudson, NY: Foundation for Economic Education.

> Bastiat was a leader of the free-trade movement that began in France in 1840. Much of what Bastiat taught is foundational to libertarian economic policy today. In this book you'll find Bastiat's often-quoted fables, *The Broken Window* and *The Petition of the Candlemakers Against the Competition of the Sun*. This is a book full of great insights in an easy-to-read style.

Bauer, P.T. (1981). *Equality, the Third World, and Economic Delusion*. Cambridge: Harvard University Press.

> Bauer, a developmental economist, shows the positive impact of capitalism on Third World countries.

Bernstein, Andrew (2005). *The Capitalist Manifesto*. Lanham, MD: University Press of America.

> Bernstein, a philosopher, does a good job summarizing the work of libertarian economists and the philosophical work of Ayn Rand. This book is a fine introductory text for objectivism, libertarianism, and capitalism.

Braudel, Fernand (1983). *The Wheels of Commerce*. New York: HarperCollins.

> Braudel, a French historian, provides evidence about the widespread destitution in pre-capitalist Europe. Charles Dickens, the novelist, tells us

that capitalism was the cause of poverty in Europe; Braudel, the historian, tells us the opposite. Read Braudel's book, then decide.

Buer, Mabel (2006). *Health, Wealth, and Population in the Early Days of the Industrial Revolution*. New York: Routledge.

The author's research uncovered dreadful evidence of unsanitary and unsafe conditions in England prior to the Industrial Revolution. She demonstrates how new technology and capitalism improved living and working conditions in the 19th century.

Caldwell, Bruce (2005). *Hayek's Challenge: An Intellectual Biography of F.A. Hayek*. Chicago: University of Chicago Press.

Caldwell, one of my colleagues at the University of North Carolina-Greensboro, is the leading authority on the work of Friedrich Hayek. Hayek was a leading thinker in the Austrian School of economics, who later wrote on social and political philosophy. Caldwell does a great job walking the reader through Hayek's journey to what is now called libertarianism.

Carson, Clarence (1991). *The War on the Poor*. Birmingham, AL: American Textbook Committee.

Professor Carson, a historian, shows how the poorest Americans have been harmed by government programs that were intended to help them.

Cassirer, Ernst (1968). *The Philosophy of the Enlightenment*. Princeton, NJ: Princeton University Press.

This is perhaps the best book on Enlightenment philosophy by a leading scholar in the field.

Cipolla, Carlo (1994). *Before the Industrial Revolution: European Society and Economy, 1000-1700* (3rd ed.). New York: W.W. Norton & Company.

The author, a renowned historian, describes the horrible living conditions in Europe before the Industrial Revolution.

Courtors, Stéphane, et. al (1999). *The Black Book of Communism: Crimes, Terror, Repression*. Cambridge, MA: Harvard University Press.

European Marxist intellectuals unemotionally discuss horrible atrocities that have been found in the archives of collapsed Eastern European communist governments. This book will convince every reader of the absolute hopelessness of a statist government (Nazi, Fascist, Socialist, or Communist) ever providing a life fit for human beings. These disastrous regimes destroyed all individual rights, individual responsibility, individual initiative, and the individuals themselves.

Fleckenstein, William (2008). *Greenspan's Bubbles: The Age of Ignorance at the Federal Reserve*. New York: McGraw Hill.

Fleckenstein, a professional money manager, uses quotes from Greenspan's speeches and congressional testimonies to show how Greenspan help create and exacerbate the two worst bubbles (stock and real estate) in American history. Greenspan's incompetence at the Federal Reserve seems inexcusable when you consider that he was once part of Ayn Rand's inner circle. Greenspan's policies led to the creation of trillions of dollars worth of derivatives, which Warren Buffett has called financial instruments of mass destruction.

Friedman, Milton & Rose (1980). *Free to Choose*. New York: Harcourt, Brace, & Company.

This was the book that opened my eyes to the importance of free markets and limited government. While I still disagree with Milton Friedman's ideas about inflating the economy, I still think this is an extraordinary book.

Hayek, Friedrich (1963). *Capitalism and Historians*. Chicago: University of Chicago Press.

The Nobel Prize-winning economist, F.A. Hayek, serves as editor of this series of essays and wrote the introductory essay. The essays are written by leading economic historians. These essays document how workers were better off after capitalism and the Industrial Revolution.

Hayek, Friedrich (2007/1944). *The Road to Serfdom*. Chicago: University of Chicago Press.

Be sure to get the 2007 edition, which is edited by Bruce Caldwell. This is Hayek's classic economic book written during World War II. John Maynard Keynes, Hayek's archrival, said it is "a grand book" and "morally and philosophically I find myself in agreement with virtually the whole of it." That's high praise from an archrival. Caldwell's 33-page introduction does a wonderful job explaining the context in which the book was written and why the book is still relevant today.

Hazlitt, Henry (1988/1946). *Economics in One Lesson*. New York: Three Rivers Press.

This is a wonderful introductory text for free market economics. Hazlitt is an excellent writer. College students should be required to read this book.

Hazlitt, Henry (1996/1973). *The Conquest of Poverty*. Irvington-on-Hudson, NY: Foundation for Economic Education.

Hazlitt shows how government programs cannot eradicate poverty or help the poor. He offers guidance on how capitalism can benefit the poor.

Hoffer, Eric (2002/1951). *The True Believer: Thoughts on the Nature of Mass Movements*. New York: Perennial Classics.

Hoffer, a self-educated genius, wrote this classic in 1951. He is amazingly insightful about human nature. The power of mass movements can be frightening. This book will help you to understand how they gain such fanatical support. If you want to protect your individual rights, read this book.

Johnson, Paul (1999). *A History of the American People*. New York: Harper Perennial.

Johnson, a British historian, describes the rise of the American nation. He attributes much of America's success to capitalism.

Mayhew, Robert (2005). *Ayn Rand Answers: The Best of Her Q&A*. New York: New American Library.

I really enjoy this exploration of Ayn Rand's mind. The depth and breadth of her knowledge is wonderfully captured in this book. Mayhew categorizes her responses in Q&A sessions and cites her countless publications. This is a great resource.

Mises, Ludwig von (2006/1956). *The Anti-Capitalist Mentality*. Indianapolis, IN: Liberty Fund.

Originally published in 1956, this is one of the best of von Mises' 25 books. Mises (1881-1973) was the leading spokesman of the Austrian School of Economics, which advocated free trade and opposed government intervention, inflation, and socialism. This book is easy to read and explains why people hate and fear capitalism. It also offers a succinct defense of capitalism.

Murray, Charles (1994). *Losing Ground: American Social Policy, 1950-1980* (10th Anniversary Edition). New York: Basic Books.

In this well-documented book, Murray (a social scientist) presents his research that shows the failures of welfare programs.

Peikoff, Leonard (1982). *The Ominous Parallels*. New York: Meridian.

Peikoff, a leading objectivist philosopher, describe the rise of Nazism in Germany in a world of philosophical turmoil. He shows the parallels in philosophical beliefs in the Weimar Republic (pre-Hitler) and today's American culture. He places much of the blame for the disastrous fascist, communist, and socialist regimes on Plato, Kant, and Hegel. I agree.

Peikoff, Leonard (1993). *Objectivism: The Philosophy of Ayn Rand*. New York: Penguin Books.

Peikoff, Ayn Rand's intellectual heir, does an excellent job walking the reader through the philosophical system of Objectivism. Objectivism is the philosophical foundation for everything in my book. I have purchased many copies for people who have not been exposed to Objectivism. They are in good hands with Peikoff.

Powell, Jim (2004). *FDR's Folly: How Roosevelt and His New Deal Prolonged the Great Depression*. New York: Three Rivers Press.

Powell, a historian, does a fine job explaining how FDR's socialist policies prolonged and exacerbated the economic problems endured by Americans during the Great Depression.

Rand, Ayn (1963). *For the New Intellectual*. New York: Signet.

In the Preface, Rand says, "I offer the present book as a lead or a summary for those who wish to acquire an integrated view of existence. They may regard it as a basic outline; it will give them the guidance they need, but only if they think through and understand the exact meaning and the full implications of these excerpts." Need I say more?

Rand Ayn (1984). *Philosophy: Who Needs It*. New York: Signet.

This collection of essays was the last work planned by Ayn Rand before her death in 1982. Rand said, "the choice we make is not whether to have a philosophy, but which one to have." Many Americans try to operate with a piecemeal approach to philosophy and ultimately end up lost.

Rand, Ayn (1986). *Capitalism: The Unknown Ideal*. New York: Signet.

This book is a series of essays on capitalism by Ayn Rand, Alan Greenspan, and Nathaniel Branden. I have recommended this book to anyone interested in the critical importance of capitalism. It is also available on audio CD.

Rand, Ayn (1999/1957). *Atlas Shrugged*. New York: Signet.

This novel, considered to be Rand's masterpiece, was originally published in 1957. Her story clearly shows what will happen if society continues on the destructive road to socialism. This popular objectivist novel will be made into a movie soon.

Rand, Ayn (2005/1943). *The Fountainhead*. New York: Signet.

In this book, originally published in 1943, Rand demonstrates her outstanding talent as a novelist, as well as a philosopher. Her leading character, architect Howard Roark, embodies the philosophy of Objectivism. Rand also demonstrated her great skills as a screenplay writer when *The Fountainhead* became a movie starring Gary Cooper, Patricia Neal, and Raymond Massey. I loved the movie.

Rand, Ayn & Peikoff, Leonard (1990). *The Voice of Reason: Essays in Objectivist Thought*. New York: Meridian.

These are wonderful essays written by Any Rand and Leonard Peikoff (her intellectual heir). I especially enjoyed Peikoff's essay entitled "My Thirty Years with Ayn Rand," which gives fascinating insight into Rand's brilliant mind.

Reisman, George (1992). *Capitalism: The Cure for Racism*. Laguna Hills, CA: The Jefferson School of Philosophy, Economics, and Psychology.

I agree with Reisman that free markets eliminate racism and ethnic bigotry; socialism and government intervention encourage hatred between groups. Reisman earned his Ph.D. under the guidance of Ludwig von Mises.

Reisman, George (1998). *Capitalism: A Treatise on Economics*. Ottawa, IL: Jameson Books.

In this thousand-page book, Reisman (an economist) presents a broad and thorough argument for free markets and free minds. He also presents devastating arguments against the anti-capitalists and anti-industrialists.

Skousen, Mark (2007). *The Big Three in Economics: Adam Smith, Karl Marx, and John Maynard Keynes*. Armonk, NY: M.E. Sharpe.

I really enjoyed this book. It is basically a history of economic thought beginning with Adam Smith. Skousen, a libertarian thinker, shows how all of the modern economists are in some way or another reacting to the economic thinking of Adam Smith. While Skousen obviously admires Smith, Skousen also points at the places in which Adam Smith was wrong.

Sowell, Thomas (1981). *Markets and Minorities*. New York: Basic Books.

Sowell, an African-American libertarian economist, demonstrates (with real-world examples) how racial minorities benefit from economic freedom and how they are harmed by government intervention.

Sowell, Thomas (1981). *Ethnic American*. New York: Basic Books.

In this book, Sowell, a scholar-in-residence at the Hoover Institute at Stanford University, focuses on the economic success of various ethnic groups. In this book, he tells how different ethnic groups have become successful. The stories are quite inspiring.

Sowell, Thomas (2003). *Applied Economics*. New York: Basic Books.

In this follow-up book to *Basic Economics*, Sowell applies the principles of free-market economics to real-world economic issues, including health care, discrimination, housing, education, etc. Sowell emphasizes the importance of understanding the long-term consequences of economic decisions.

Sowell, Thomas (2007). *Basic Economics*, Third Edition. New York: Basic Books.

In this book, Sowell does an excellent job of discussing a wide range of economic issues from a libertarian viewpoint. He helps the reader understand the importance of the incentives created by a program, rather than the intent. Like all of Sowell's work, I highly recommend this book.

Stossel, John (2005). *Give Me a Break*. New York: HarperCollins.

ABC's 20/20 anchor, John Stossel talks about his 30-year journalism career that took him from left-wing social beliefs to libertarianism. Stossel's concrete examples show the critical importance of capitalism, free markets, and free minds. You can also find Stossel's work on Harper Audio and on the ABC 20/20 website.

Stossel, John (2007). *Myths, Lies, and Downright Stupidity: Get Out the Shovel-Why Everything You Know is Wrong*. New York: Hyperion.

In this book, Stossel does a great job exploding the myths about big government, public schools, the media, and health care. This book is also available in audio CD. The issues are serious, but Stossel will make you laugh at the absurdity.

Tanner, Michael (1996). *The End of Welfare: Fighting Poverty in the Civil Society*. Washington, DC: The Cato Institute.

You can purchase this book from the Cato Institute for $5. Tanner, the Director of Health & Welfare Studies at the Cato Institute (a libertarian think tank), traces the history of welfare programs and finds their roots in the Progressive Era, which lead to the New Deal and the Great Society. Tanner believes the thinking of both liberals and conservatives is flawed concerning welfare. He suggests two changes. First, reduce government regulation and taxation so that the economy is allowed to grow. Second, rely on private charities (after reducing regulations and taxation) to assist individuals who cannot work. Phyllis Berry Myers, of the Center for New Black Leadership, says "this book is a must read." I agree.

Williams, Walter (1982). *The State Against Blacks*. New York: McGraw-Hill.

Williams, an African-American professor, argues that government interventions have hindered, not helped, African-Americans. Professor Williams has been a vocal advocate for free markets for more than 25 years.

Williams, Walter (1999). *More Liberty Means Less Government*. Stanford, CA: Hoover Institute Press.

In this collection of essays, Professor Williams (a libertarian) speaks bluntly about a variety of social and political issues. This book includes many of his favorite previously published newspaper columns.

Yergin, Daniel & Stanislaw, Joseph (1998). *The Commanding Heights: The Battle Between Government and the Marketplace that is Remaking the Modern World*. New York: Touchstone Books.

Yergin and Stanislaw discuss the worldwide movement toward privatization and free markets. This book has also been made into an excellent video.

About the Author

Dr. Michael Beitler (pronounced Bite-ler) is an advocate for individual rights, limited government, and free markets. Mike has been recognized as a leading business executive, business professor, consultant, and author. Dr. Beitler's book, *Strategic Organizational Change*, is required reading in MBA programs worldwide. Mike's DVD, *Overcoming Resistance to Change*, has been ranked #1 business video on Amazon.com.

Mike was a candidate for the US Senate in 2010. His radio show, *"Free Markets,"* airs live on the VoiceAmerica Business Network.

Mike can be reached at mike@mikebeitler.com.